RESILIENT

Copyright © 2024 by Ethan R. Esbach.

All rights reserved. No part of this book may be used or reproduced without written permission, except for brief quotations in critical articles or reviews. Printed in the South Africa

For more information or to order books or book a keynote address, contact :
Ethan R. Esbach Holdings (Pty) Ltd

Cell Number 084 234 4090
E-mail – info@ethanresbach.com
Website – ethanresbach.com

ISBN - Hardcover: 978-0-7961-6793-4
ISBN – e-book: 978-0-7961–6794-1

First Edition: May 2024

RESILIENT

POWERFUL LESSON
*For Turning Your Adversity
Into Extraordinary Success*

ETHAN R. ESBACH

ABOUT THE AUTHOR

Ethan R. Esbach is a dynamic force in the business world. He drives change and expands his enterprises to set up a global presence. Having both qualifications in Mechanical and Electrical Engineering, he brings a wealth of experience in Mechanical and Electrical Engineering, Entrepreneurship, Sales, and Marketing. With his diverse ability, Ethan R. Esbach is committed to empowering individuals and delivering world-class solutions tailored to their needs.

He has collaborated with manufacturing plants to improve production assembly, engineering design, drawing offices, and marketing corporations to advise and enhance their strategies. Through Esbach Transport, Ethan supports the film industry by providing vehicles for large production companies. His experience uniquely positions him to empower you to reach your full potential.

As Director of Ethan R. Esbach Holdings, he maximizes each employee's growth by helping their skills develop. As a motivational speaker, Ethan is committed to providing listeners with practical, up-to-date information and easy-to-understand principles that are proven to work.

His talks are broadcast live from various conferences, book launches, and graduation ceremonies, ensuring their relevance and impact. As the author of his new book, he is the epitome of resilience; he has meticulously designed a comprehensive succession plan for all those dedicated to reaching their full potential. Through his coaching program "Resilient," he has curated a transformative guide that seamlessly blends the wisdom of RESILIENT with a collection of tools all aimed at nurturing personal growth!

ACKNOWLEDGMENTS

Thanks to my father, George Esbach, for embodying resilience and teaching us valuable lessons about transforming adversity into extraordinary success through this book. May his guidance inspire us to persevere and never give up!

Thank you, Daddy, for showing me your most incredible power when you were the weakest. I value your life lessons and appreciate the wisdom you shared over many years of our partnership, strong friendship, and building a bond so strong we will forever remain teammates, even when all will be left will be memories.

Thank you, Daddy, for investing in me and helping me understand my total capacity to love and the power of God's love, which will remain the most remarkable presence in my life.

TABLE OF CONTENTS

LESSON 0: Starting Point - Starting At the Beginning	1
LESSON 1: Resilient Mindset - Understanding Resilience in Business	5
LESSON 2: Confronting Self Doubt - Building A Strong Foundation for Resilience	39
LESSON 3: Its Technically Technical Strategies - Strategies for Overcoming Adversity	49
LESSON 4: Leading Resiliently - Cultivating Resilience in Leadership	99
LESSON 5: Sustainablity Leads to Resilience - Resilience In the Long run	149
LESSON 6: I Have Failed - Maintaining a Positive Mindset	187
LESSON 7: Fair and Square - Unmasking the Inner Critic	199
REFERENCES	209

LESSON 0

Starting Point

Starting At the Beginning

Welcome to "Resilient - Powerful Lessons for Turning Your Adversity Into Extraordinary Success," a book I thoroughly enjoyed planning and writing based on my practical experience. As an entrepreneur, I realized that certain aspects of starting and running a business were not as easy as they seemed without proper guidance and experience. The advice I needed, or guidance came at a high price, which formed some of the bases of this book, and I trust the guidance enriches your ability to stay positive during challenging times.

STARTING POINT

> *"When we begin to move toward our purpose in life, we realize that our frequency begins to disrupt others who vibrate in discontinuity."*
>
> — ETHAN R. ESBACH

Everything has a beginning

The unique experience and distinctive smell of a book's pages trigger a profound satisfaction as I reflect on the transformative power of words and paragraphs. These written expressions can provide practical value to those who engage with them. This book is not just a collection of words but a valuable resource for personal and business growth, offering practical advice and strategies to empower you. I am excited to share it with you, knowing it will equip you with the necessary tools for your journey. I aim to benefit those who know me, and if not, I hope it will positively influence a broader audience.

Resilient reveals how resilience has become a powerful tool for achieving success in the business world. The examples, stories, and advice in this book have taken many years to develop. I tested and refined these tools until the blueprint was good enough to share with you, whom I have not met worldwide, not even you, my closest. I write this book not as an expert in everything resilience but as a fellow traveller on personal and business growth. I value your journey and hope to contribute to your growth. Within these pages, I have chronicled the vision, processing, and implementing lessons that have characterized my entrepreneurial journey. I take a lesson approach to teaching concepts I have mastered over the years while sharing my life's resilience. I hope that by sharing my journey, you will feel connected and inspired to embark on your path of resilience and growth.

Resilience has been a defining trait in my life, a testament to the power of determination. This book is my way of passing on that empowerment and guidance to the reader. I have made many mistakes on my journey to becoming a successful, still-growing entrepreneur, and I hope to share these lessons with you — a source of guidance and a place to draw encouragement during the most challenging times.

My approach to this book is not only to seek that it be a reference manual for many or a source of light or information but also to meet those readers who seek more than advice but seek to know the author and find inspiration through the stories shared. I hope this book will reassure and guide you in your personal and business growth as a reliable companion on your journey. Many people never get the chance to publish a book that serves as both a self-help guide and a way to establish a connection with individuals who may need mentorship. This book is an opportunity to get to know the author more deeply. In today's world, we often focus on end-time events, but despite that, we are still encouraged to live fulfilling lives. Even though this sounds possible with the least effort, that is far from the truth. We all have our dreams and purposes, and I hope this book helps you find or help you to live within your purpose.

> Welcome to "Resilient - Powerful Lessons For Turning Your Adversity Into Extraordinary Success," a book I thoroughly enjoyed planning and writing based on my practical experience. As an entrepreneur, I realized that certain aspects of starting and running a business were not

as easy as they seemed without proper guidance and experience. The advice I needed, or guidance came at a high price, which formed some of the bases of this book, and I trust the guidance enriches your ability to stay positive during challenging times.

The lessons you, as the reader, will experience are the ones I have been taught and the ones I have learned about how to become more resilient in the face of obstacles. My advice is based on specific personal experiences in business. This book has been a self-funded project that taught me that anything is possible if your desire is greater than the obstacles you are facing. Drawing from real-life experiences, I have written this book so that you can envision your passion as not in the mind or heart but as a practical everyday enjoyment to be part of.

With this book's transformational power, I present resilience in the business world and life in a way that speaks to the Navy Seal living within you: yes, you! We must only unlock the greatest within us by believing we can obtain our uniquely written stories. We are driven but uninspired, and in today's world, a powerful transformation is required to build more resilient people to manage resilient businesses and to, in the end, live purposeful lives that contribute to society, your community, and your legacy.

I begin to encourage you by digging into the very understanding of resilience since many understand resilience as being in adverse situations. However, no one can define a way about the aspect, around, over, or underneath, in a manner that brings hope and shines the light on an already existing greatness rather than having to source tons of resources. Resilient is an essential guide only; for a more comprehensive guide, I have a coaching program to formulate your unique resilience and help empower its growth.

LESSON 1

Resilient Mindset

Understanding Resilience in Business

To develop a resilient mindset for race day, we must first know how to manage pressure effectively and find ways to stay motivated and focused on our goals. For instance, business owners face familiar challenges such as time management, providing continuous value, and adapting marketing strategies. All these factors are related to developing a resilient mindset, which leads to creating a plan for managing these challenges.

> *"Mindset is a concept that can be taught, but taking action is a decision."*
>
> – ETHAN R. ESBACH

The Importance of Resilience in Business

Resilience is not just a trait but an influential tool business owners can use to navigate the ever-changing entrepreneurship landscape. In the face of adversity, setbacks, and failures, resilience empowers individuals to bounce back, learn from their experiences, and grow more robust. Without resilience, it is easy to become discouraged and give up when faced with challenges. In the business world, where uncertainty is a constant, having a resilient mindset can make all the difference in achieving success, giving business owners a sense of control and capability.

When I started my journey as an entrepreneur, I was unsure how to do things, as no one or an institution had given me formal training. However, I found myself in the position of building my rocket on my way upwards. Well, not having any wings, I guess it was on its way to no man's land. Theoretically, this sounds fabulous, or at least the rocket part did, but putting the words into practice or drafted concepts required another set of skills and tools, some of which are born with and, in some cases, taught.

One critical reason resilience is essential in business is that it allows individuals to adapt to change. In today's fast-paced world, companies must be able to pivot quickly in response to market trends, technological advancements, and other external factors. Resilient people are better equipped to handle unexpected changes and setbacks and are likelier to come out on top. By embracing challenges and setbacks as opportunities for growth, resilient business owners can position themselves for long-term success.

Some strategies for building resilience include preparing for the unexpected by organizing your processes into manageable tasks, and others could be working on adaptability when circumstances change. What a mouthful. I know these things are not rocket science, but it does come close. Let me break it down simply for you. The person who can genuinely survive as an entrepreneur with long-term success, regardless of the size of your business, must have a vision that will keep them going and the mindset to navigate the obstacles.

> A mindset without vision is only positive thinking, but a vision without a mindset is only dreams. When embodied together, it can empower a chain of events to the benefit of the entrepreneur and many for whom the value is created. Resilience is not just about business success but personal growth and development. I had no idea in my 14-year-old mind that I would become an entrepreneur in years to come. My mindset was to follow the nine-to-five and hope I would find my joy. I knew I would stream into visions and goals that would reward my efforts for trying differently. As business owners face obstacles and setbacks, they can learn valuable lessons that can help them improve their skills, strategies, and decision-making abilities.

By developing a resilient mindset, individuals can cultivate a growth mindset that allows them to see setbacks as opportunities for learning and growth rather than failures. This ability to bounce back from adversity and continue moving forward is essential for business success and personal development, inspiring and motivating business owners to develop this trait. I must add that resilience is not just a trait but a competitive advantage in the marketplace. In an increasingly competitive business environment, perseverance in the face of challenges can set individuals apart from their competitors. Resilient business owners can stay focused on their goals, adapt to changing circumstances, and overcome obstacles with grace and determination. Did I mention determination? We have heard this word before, but how does determination guarantee an empire that can withstand?

This determination can inspire confidence in employees, customers, and other stakeholders and help businesses stand out in a crowded market, giving business owners a strong sense of reassurance and confidence. How better would it be as you grow your business to flourish so that it stands out boldly, marking its vision? The importance of resilience in business cannot be overstated. I am sure this book would not have been possible if determination was not a word, I was willing to unpack. Ultimately, resilience is crucial for personal growth and development and business success.

Common Challenges Faced by Business Owners

As business owners, we must acknowledge and address the common challenges we face in our journey to success. These challenges can often feel overwhelming, but we can overcome them by developing a resilient mindset and continuing to grow and thrive in our businesses.

I want to highlight and explore some of the most common challenges business owners face and discuss strategies for overcoming them. One joint challenge is the constant pressure to succeed. Man, oh man, was I hungry to get to the top, but at the expense of little to no sleep, I found myself crashing while at the same time losing my ability to meet the demands I had promised. That is one setback or failure group no true entrepreneur wants to experience.

Running a business requires a lot of time, effort, and dedication, and it can be easy to feel overwhelmed by the weight of these responsibilities. Chasing the American dream has pros and cons, but before diving into the purpose of chasing, I want to revise the thought with you on running up the mountain without having a training program fit for race day. In the same mindset of chasing, chaise one day at a time means to plan, reveal, recheck, and confirm that the goal of finishing is still in sight.

> To develop a resilient mindset for race day, we must first know how to manage pressure effectively and find ways to stay motivated and focused on our goals. For instance, business owners face familiar challenges such as time management, providing continuous value, and adapting marketing strategies. All these factors are related to developing a resilient mindset, which leads to creating a plan for managing these challenges.

We have never heard an entrepreneur say, "Today is a great day to fail and be unproductive, unsuccessful, and lazy." If that were the case, we would all be using Morse code to communicate or send messages via pigeons with notes attached to their feet instead of using email or walking instead of driving. During this timeline, an entrepreneur needed to identify the problem and develop a plan to create the value we use today.

Another challenge that many businesses owners face is dealing with uncertainty and unpredictability. The business world is constantly changing, and it can be difficult to predict what challenges or opportunities may arise in the future. By cultivating a resilient mindset, we can embrace uncertainty and adapt to changes as they come rather than letting them derail our progress or even allow external challenges, such as when business owners face internal obstacles such as self-doubt and fear of failure.

I remember how often I doubted myself, wondering if I was driving impact correctly if I had a sustaining business model, or if I would need to develop a new one, am I was being judged for how I do things; these negative thoughts and emotions can hold us back from taking risks and pursuing our goals with confidence. By creating a resilient mindset, we can learn to overcome these internal barriers and cultivate a sense of self-belief and determination that will drive us forward in our businesses.

Recognizing and addressing common challenges that business owners face is essential. These challenges can sometimes be easy to detect, while other times they may become larger issues that need to be dealt with later. By developing the resilience needed to navigate the highs and lows of entrepreneurship, we can build a solid mindset and adopt strategies to manage stress, uncertainty, and self-doubt.

This will help us overcome obstacles and continue to grow and succeed in our businesses. With a resilient mindset, we can confront challenges directly and emerge stronger and more determined. Staying motivated is not easy, but it's important to acknowledge these challenges and take action to address them rather than delay.

The Benefits of Developing a Resilient Mindset

In the fast-paced and competitive business world, challenges and setbacks are inevitable. However, their ability to develop a resilient mindset sets successful business owners apart. This is the ability to bounce back from adversity, stay focused on long-term goals, and maintain a positive outlook despite obstacles. I expand on the benefits of developing a resilient mindset and how it can help business owners overcome challenges and succeed.

One key benefit of developing a resilient mindset is increased mental toughness. While resilience is the ability to bounce back from adversity, mental toughness is the ability to stay focused on long-term goals and maintain a positive outlook despite obstacles. Business owners with a resilient mindset are better equipped to handle the stress and pressure of running a business.

Any company's day-to-day activities can become time-consuming, and energy often runs low occasionally. Still, when these daily activities form part of the long-term plan, the smaller milestones reached on the way help create a sense of achievement. They can stay calm and focused on high-pressure situations, make decisions quickly and effectively, and easily adapt to changing circumstances. This mental toughness is vital for navigating the ups and downs of the business world and coming out stronger on the other side.

Another benefit of developing a resilient mindset is improved problem-solving skills. Resilient business owners approach the situation clearly and rationally when faced with a challenge or setback. They see the bigger picture, identify potential solutions, and take decisive action to address the issue. This ability to think critically and problem-solve effectively is crucial for overcoming obstacles and finding creative solutions to complex problems.

I must admit that developing a resilient mindset can lead to increased emotional intelligence. Therefore, resilient business owners can better manage their emotions, communicate effectively with others, and build strong relationships with employees, clients, and partners.

This emotional intelligence allows them to create a positive work environment, inspire and motivate their team, and foster a culture of collaboration and innovation within their organization. Ultimately, this can increase productivity, employee satisfaction, and overall business success.

For example, a resilient business owner might want to focus on positivity and emotional insight within their organization or even drive teams to excel with self-development plans to help build the organization's workforce and improve quality control. By taking a positive stance at work, employees can adapt to adversity and hold on to a sense of control over their work environment.

Putting energy and motivation into work or having 'vigour' – as described by Shirom (2004) – is also associated with building personal resilience. It is the 'opposite' of burnout, characterized by emotional exhaustion, physical tiredness, and cognitive or 'weariness.' Vigor is characterized by having the capacity to put in the maximum effort at work and thus further build personal resilience (Shirom, 2004).

Another example of building personal resilience at work is developing and strengthening emotional insight. Insight is closely related to emotional intelligence. Individuals with a level of understanding are aware of the full range of emotions they experience, from 'negative' to 'positive.'

They will also consider the ramifications of their reactions and behaviour and the effects of their actions on others. Psychologically resilient individuals can be described as emotionally intelligent (Tugade & Fredrickson, 2004).

Emotional intelligence encompasses much more than what Resilient as a book mentions. Daniel Goleman has written a book on this topic to explore it further. In addition, a resilient mindset can also have a positive impact on personal growth and development.

Business owners who develop resilience are more likely to embrace challenges as opportunities for growth and learning. They are open to new experiences, willing to take risks, and constantly seeking ways to improve themselves and their business. This continuous growth and development mindset can increase confidence, self-awareness, and fulfillment in their personal and professional lives.

A resilient mindset is essential for business owners who want to overcome challenges, succeed, and thrive in today's competitive business environment. By cultivating mental toughness, improving problem-solving skills, enhancing emotional intelligence, and embracing personal growth and development, business owners can position themselves for long-term success and create a lasting impact in their industry.

So, take the time to develop a resilient mindset and watch as your business grows and flourishes in the face of adversity. "There are no better opportunities than the ones you have right now! Right now is not just a moment on your journey; it is when you need to discover your greatest strength in the face of your lowest and highest disappointments."

Understanding Resilience

Resilience stands as a potent trait that empowers individuals to conquer obstacles and achieve success in their lives. It is the capacity to rebound from setbacks, adapt to change, and advance despite challenges. Comprehending resilience is paramount to harnessing and leveraging its power for one's benefit. A pivotal facet of resilience is maintaining a positive mindset in adversity.

This involves viewing challenges as opportunities for growth and learning rather than insurmountable obstacles. Individuals can fortify the mental resilience needed to persevere through tough times and emerge even stronger by cultivating a positive attitude.

Another crucial element of resilience is the ability to adapt to change. Life is teeming with unexpected twists and turns, and being capable of rolling with the punches is imperative for success. Resilient individuals can embrace change, learn from their experiences, and adjust their plans accordingly. This flexibility empowers them to navigate challenges gracefully and emerge victorious.

Resilience also encompasses developing robust coping skills and healthy coping mechanisms for dealing with stress. This includes prioritizing self-care, seeking support from friends and family, and finding channels for emotional expression. By tending to their well-being and reaching out for assistance when needed, individuals can cultivate the resilience required to weather any storm.

Understanding resilience is indispensable for surmounting obstacles and attaining success. By nurturing a positive mindset, adapting to change, and honing strong coping skills, individuals can harness resilience to transform adversity into unparalleled success. With unwavering determination and perseverance, anyone can tap into their inner strength and conquer whatever challenges come their way.

Building Resilience Skills

Building resilience skills is developing robust coping mechanisms. This involves learning to manage stress, regulate emotions, and solve problems effectively. By honing these skills, individuals can better navigate the ups and downs of life and maintain a sense of balance and well-being.

Resilience skills include cultivating a robust support system. Surrounding oneself with positive, encouraging people who lift you during tough times can make all the difference. Whether it is friends, family, or a mentor, having a support system in place can provide a sense of security and comfort during challenging times. Having these skills is crucial to achieving success and overcoming obstacles.

By developing a positive mindset, robust coping mechanisms, and a supportive network, individuals can build the resilience they need to face life's challenges head-on and emerge more vital than ever before. With determination, perseverance, and a commitment to growth, anyone can turn adversity into extraordinary success.

The Importance of Resilience in Achieving Success

Achieving success, regardless of your age, and being resilient in your attempts at success means you are finding your challenges necessary. It is the ability to bounce back from setbacks, challenges, and failures and keep moving towards your goals. Without resilience, it is easy to become discouraged and give up when faced with obstacles. However, with resilience, you can overcome adversity and turn it into an opportunity for growth and success.

In today's fast-paced and competitive world, resilience is more important than ever. Successful individuals are set apart by their ability to adapt to change, learn from failures, and keep pushing forward. Whether you are just starting your career or are well into retirement, developing resilience is essential for achieving your goals and reaching your full potential.

One of the most critical aspects of resilience is having a positive mindset. Instead of dwelling on past failures or setbacks, resilient individuals focus on what they can learn from the experience and how to improve. By maintaining a positive attitude, you can overcome any obstacle that comes your way and continue to move towards your goals with confidence and determination.

Another critical component of resilience is the ability to adapt to change. In today's rapidly changing world, pivoting and adjusting one's plans is essential for success. Resilient individuals are flexible and open to new opportunities, allowing them to navigate challenges and setbacks easily. By embracing change and staying adaptable, you can position yourself for success in any situation.

It is not only a powerful trait that can help you overcome any obstacle and achieve extraordinary success at any age, but by developing a positive mindset, embracing change, and never giving up on your goals, you can turn adversity into opportunity and reach your full potential. Remember, your challenges do not determine success; it depends on how you respond to them. Stay resilient, stay determined, and you will achieve greatness.

Finding Your Obstacles

One of the first steps in overcoming obstacles and achieving success is identifying the challenges in your way. I remember one of my most significant challenges was trying to complete a degree above my capacity to manage because I had made too many excuses for why it was okay to fail. By examining your obstacles closely, you can develop a plan for overcoming them. This process requires self-awareness and honesty about the barriers holding you back. Although confronting these obstacles may be uncomfortable, it is a necessary step toward resilience and success. When identifying your obstacles, it is essential to consider both external and internal factors.

External obstacles are the challenges that come from outside sources, such as financial limitations, societal expectations, or geographic location. On the other hand, internal obstacles are the barriers that come from within yourself, such as self-doubt, fear of failure, or lack of motivation. By recognizing both types of obstacles, you can begin to address them with a comprehensive approach.

One powerful way to identify your obstacles is to reflect on past experiences and patterns in your life. Look back on moments when you faced difficulties or setbacks, and consider what factors contributed to those challenges. By identifying recurring themes or patterns, you can gain insight into the obstacles that may continue to arise in your path to success. This reflection can help you to develop strategies for overcoming these obstacles in the future.

Another critical aspect of identifying your obstacles is seeking feedback from others. Sometimes, we may not see our obstacles clearly, but others may be able to provide valuable insight. Contact trusted friends, mentors, or coaches and ask for their perspectives on your challenges. Their feedback can help you gain new perspectives and identify obstacles to consider.

Identifying your obstacles is crucial in the journey to resilience and success. By reflecting on your challenges, considering external and internal factors, and seeking feedback from others, you can clearly understand the barriers that stand in your way. With this awareness, you can create a plan for overcoming these obstacles and achieving your goals. Remember, obstacles are not roadblocks but opportunities for growth and transformation. Embrace the challenges ahead and use them as stepping stones to reach extraordinary success.

Developing a Resilient Mindset

This subchapter will explore the key components of developing a resilient mindset to overcome obstacles and achieve success. Resilience is the ability to bounce back from setbacks and challenges, and it is a crucial skill to cultivate in today's fast-paced world. By developing a resilient mindset, individuals can survive difficult times, thrive, and grow more robust in the face of adversity.

One of the first steps in developing a resilient mindset is cultivating a positive attitude. This means focusing on the silver lining in every situation and looking for opportunities for growth and learning. By adopting a positive mindset, individuals can reframe setbacks as opportunities for personal development and self-improvement.

Another critical aspect of developing a resilient mindset is to practice self-care and self-compassion. Taking care of oneself physically, emotionally, and mentally is essential to build resilience. This includes getting enough rest, eating well, exercising regularly, and seeking support from friends and loved ones.

By prioritizing self-care, individuals can better cope with stress and bounce back from challenges more easily. In addition to self-care, it is essential to cultivate a growth mindset. This involves believing in one's ability to learn and grow, even in the face of failure. By embracing a growth mindset, individuals can view setbacks as opportunities for learning and improvement rather than insurmountable obstacles. This mindset shift can help individuals build resilience and progress toward their goals, even in adversity.

Finally, developing a resilient mindset also involves practicing gratitude and mindfulness. By focusing on the present moment and appreciating the good things in life, individuals can cultivate a sense of perspective and resilience.

Gratitude can help individuals stay positive and hopeful, even in the face of challenges, while mindfulness can help individuals remain grounded and centred in the present moment. By incorporating these practices into their daily lives, individuals can build a resilient mindset that will serve them well in overcoming obstacles and reaching success.

Strategies for Overcoming Obstacles

In life, we are bound to face obstacles and challenges that can sometimes seem impossible. However, it is essential to remember that with the right mindset and strategies, we can overcome any adversity that comes our way. This subchapter will explore practical techniques for overcoming obstacles and reaching success, regardless of age.

Maintaining a positive attitude is one of the most important strategies for overcoming obstacles. When faced with challenges, it can be easy to get bogged down by negative thoughts and emotions. Still, you can overcome even the most formidable barriers by staying positive and focusing on solutions rather than problems. Remember that setbacks are a part of life and can often lead to new opportunities for growth and success.

Another key strategy for overcoming obstacles is to set clear goals and create a plan of action. By breaking down your goals into smaller, manageable steps, you can progress towards overcoming barriers one step at a time. This will help you stay motivated and focused on the end goal, even when faced with setbacks or challenges.

Additionally, it is essential to cultivate a robust support system of friends, family, and mentors who can provide encouragement and guidance during difficult times. Surrounding yourself with positive influences can help you stay motivated and inspired to overcome obstacles and succeed. Be bold and seek help when needed, as having a solid support system can make all the difference in overcoming challenges.

Finally, practicing self-care and prioritizing your physical and mental well-being when facing obstacles is crucial. Taking care of yourself through exercise, healthy eating, and relaxation techniques can help you stay resilient and focused when overcoming challenges. Remember that you can overcome any obstacle that comes your way, and with the right strategies and mindset, you can turn adversity into extraordinary success at any age.

Embracing Failure as a Learning Opportunity

Failure is often seen as a negative experience, but it can be one of the most significant opportunities for growth and learning. Embracing failure as a learning opportunity is essential for building resilience and reaching success. When we view failure as a stepping stone rather than a roadblock, we open ourselves to a world of possibilities and potential.

> One of the most essential lessons from failure is that it is not the end of the road but rather a detour on the path to success. Failure can provide valuable insights into what went wrong and how we can improve. We can turn setbacks into stepping stones toward our goals by embracing failure as a learning opportunity. It is also important to remember that failure is a natural learning process. No one achieves success without facing failure along the way. By reframing our perspective on failure and seeing it as an opportunity for growth, we can develop the resilience needed to overcome obstacles and reach our full potential.

When we embrace failure as a learning opportunity, we also open ourselves to new possibilities and experiences. Failure can catalyse change and innovation, pushing us to think outside the box and explore new ways of approaching challenges. By embracing failure, we can tap into our creativity and resilience to overcome obstacles and achieve extraordinary success.

Embracing failure as a learning opportunity is a powerful mindset shift that can lead to incredible personal growth and success. By reframing our perspective on failure and seeing it as a stepping stone towards our goals, we can build resilience, develop new skills, and reach our full potential. Whether you are 18 or 90, the lessons learned from embracing failure will help you turn adversity into extraordinary success.

Finding Strength in Adversity

Life consists of challenges and obstacles that can test our resilience and strength. However, during these times of adversity, we can dig deep and find the inner strength we never knew we had. We can grow, learn, and ultimately become stronger individuals in adversity. It is through overcoming these obstacles that we can truly reach success. One of the most powerful lessons from adversity is the importance of staying positive and maintaining a hopeful outlook. When faced with challenges, it can be easy to become overwhelmed and lose sight of the bigger picture. However, by focusing on the positive aspects of the situation and believing in our ability to overcome it, we can find the strength to persevere.

It is important to remember that every obstacle is an opportunity for growth and self-discovery. Another critical lesson in finding strength in adversity is the value of resilience. Resilience is the ability to bounce back from setbacks and progress despite obstacles. By cultivating resilience, we can develop the mental toughness and perseverance needed to overcome any challenge that comes our way. It is through resilience that we can turn our adversity into extraordinary success.

In addition to staying positive and cultivating resilience, seeking support from others during adversity is also essential. Surrounding ourselves with a robust support system of friends, family, and mentors can give us the encouragement and guidance to navigate difficult times. By leaning on others for support, we can gain valuable insights and perspectives to help us overcome obstacles and grow stronger.

Ultimately, finding strength in adversity is about embracing the challenges that come our way and using them as opportunities for growth and self-improvement. By maintaining a positive outlook, cultivating resilience, and seeking support from others, we can turn our adversity into extraordinary success. It is through facing and overcoming obstacles that we can truly reach our full potential and achieve greatness in life.

Using Adversity to Fuel Your Success

Adversity is an inevitable part of life, but how we respond to it can make all the difference in our journey toward success. In this subchapter, we will explore using adversity to fuel your success and how you can harness the power of resilience to overcome obstacles and achieve your goals.

> By shifting your perspective and viewing challenges as opportunities for growth and learning, you can turn setbacks into stepping stones toward a brighter future. One fundamental way to use adversity to fuel your success is to embrace the lessons that come with difficult experiences. Instead of viewing setbacks as failures, see them as valuable opportunities to learn and grow.

By reflecting on your challenges and identifying the lessons they have taught you, you can gain valuable insights that will help you navigate future obstacles with confidence and resilience. Another powerful way to use adversity to fuel your success is by cultivating a growth mindset. Instead of viewing setbacks as permanent roadblocks, see them as temporary hurdles that can be overcome with perseverance and determination.

Adopting an attitude that values effort and persistence can turn adversity into a personal and professional growth catalyst. Embracing the belief that you can learn and improve from every challenge will empower you to face obstacles head-on and emerge stronger on the other side. So, embracing the lessons, cultivating a growth mindset, and seeking support from others during times of adversity is essential. Surrounding yourself with a strong support network of friends, family, mentors, and colleagues can give you the encouragement, guidance, and perspective you need to navigate difficult times.

By sharing your experiences and seeking advice from those who have faced similar challenges, you can gain valuable insights and strategies for overcoming adversity and achieving success. Ultimately, using adversity to fuel your success is about harnessing the power of resilience to overcome obstacles and achieve your goals.

By embracing the lessons, cultivating a growth mindset, and seeking support from others, you can transform setbacks into opportunities for growth and personal development. Remember that adversity is not a roadblock but a stepping stone towards a brighter future. With the right mindset and support system, you can turn your adversity into extraordinary success and emerge stronger, wiser, and more resilient than ever before.

Learning from Resilient Individuals

In the subchapter "Learning from Resilient Individuals," we will explore the stories of individuals who have overcome tremendous obstacles to achieve success. These resilient individuals are potent examples of how to turn adversity into opportunity and triumph.

Examining their journeys can give us valuable insights and inspiration to navigate our challenges and setbacks. One such individual is Malala

Yousafzai, the Pakistani education activist who survived a brutal attack by the Taliban for advocating for girls' education. Despite facing death threats and violence, Malala remained steadfast in her mission and became the youngest-ever Nobel Prize laureate. Her resilience in the face of adversity serves as a reminder of the power of courage and determination in achieving one's goals.

Another inspiring figure is Nick Vujicic, a motivational speaker born without arms and legs. Despite his physical limitations, Nick has travelled the world sharing his message of hope and perseverance. His story teaches us that true resilience comes from within, and that no obstacle is too significant to overcome with the right mindset and attitude.

We can also learn valuable lessons from Oprah Winfrey, who rose from a difficult childhood marked by poverty and abuse to become one of the most successful media moguls in the world. Oprah's resilience and unwavering determination to succeed testify to the transformative power of perseverance and self-belief.

By studying the stories of these resilient individuals, we can gain insights into the traits that enable them to overcome adversity and achieve extraordinary success. Their experiences remind us that setbacks and challenges are not roadblocks but opportunities for growth and transformation. With the right mindset and determination, we, too, can turn our struggles into stepping stones towards a brighter future.

Cultivating Resilience in Your Daily Life

Cultivating resilience in daily life is an essential skill for navigating the ups and downs that come your way. Resilience is the ability to bounce back from setbacks, adapt to change, and progress despite challenges. To cultivate resilience, it is important to develop a positive mindset and practice self-care. By taking care of your physical, emotional, and mental well-being, you can better cope with stress and adversity.

One powerful way to cultivate resilience in your daily life is to practice gratitude. By focusing on what you are grateful for, you can shift your perspective from what is going wrong to what is going right. This can help you build a sense of optimism and hope, even in the face of adversity. By acknowledging the good in your life, you can build your resilience muscle and develop a more positive outlook on life. Another key aspect of cultivating resilience is building a solid support network. Surrounding yourself with positive, supportive people can help you weather the storms of life and provide you with the encouragement and guidance you need to keep going. Whether it is family, friends, or a mentor, having people in your corner who believe in you and your ability to overcome challenges can make all the difference in your resilience journey.

To practice gratitude and build a support network, it is important to develop a growth mindset. This means viewing challenges as opportunities for growth and learning rather than insurmountable obstacles. By embracing a growth mindset, you can approach setbacks with curiosity and determination, knowing you have the power to learn and grow from every experience.

Overall, cultivating resilience in your daily life is a practice that takes time and effort, but the rewards are well worth it. You can navigate life's challenges with grace and resilience by developing a positive mindset, practicing self-care, cultivating gratitude, building a support network, and embracing a growth mindset. Remember, resilience is not about avoiding obstacles but facing them head-on and emerging more substantially on the other side.

Celebrating Your Resilience Victories

As I look back to the moment I woke up for the very first time, I woke up in a sterile hospital room with a profound sense of disorientation. My last memory was of the evening I said good night to my father; we were both so consumed by the symptoms of COVID that stats read no chance of another chance, but now I was being told that I had been in a coma for two long months due to complications from COVID-19.

It was a jolt to my system, a surreal twist of fate that I struggled to understand—so much time had slipped away, leaving me to grapple with the reality of it all. As I slowly drifted back to consciousness, I began to understand the extent of my losses. My legs were unresponsive, my speech slurred, and even holding a pen seemed an insurmountable challenge. Simple tasks I had once taken for granted now felt like monumental obstacles. I felt like a baby, relearning everything from the ground up.

The physical therapy was grueling, but I was determined not to let this setback define me. Every day, I pushed myself to take a step, pronounce one more word, and hold the pen steadily. It was frustrating and exhausting, but I refused to give up. What I hated the most about rehabilitation was the consistency of the exercises you needed to do so that the body could become used to movements again. What a nightmare! I felt like baby Ethan crawling at age 34. One cannot understand the need to stay positive in doubt or confusion.

With the unwavering support of my family, friends, and the resolute hospital staff, I began to glimpse a flicker of hope. Their encouragement and belief in me were the fuel that propelled me forward. Each small step was a monumental victory, no matter how insignificant it seemed. Learning to walk again, I wanted to scale a mountain, and being able to print my name, I wished to cross the marathon finish line.

There were moments of doubt and despair when I feared I would never be the same again.

Nevertheless, I clung to the hope of reclaiming my former life with hard work and determination. I refused to let COVID-19 rob me of my future. Months crept by, and progress was slow, but it was there. I could feel the strength returning to my muscles, my speech becoming more precise, and my handwriting steadily improving. It was a long and arduous journey, but every step forward filled me with pride and resolve.

Finally, after an eternity, I took my first unassisted steps. The tears of joy in my family's eyes reflected my overwhelming sense of accomplishment and relief. I had conquered the impossible and appeared even stronger than before. Today, I can walk, talk, write, read, and be active, just like I used to before the coma caused by COVID-19. Every step I take and every word I speak constantly reminds me of the resilience and inner strength that brought me through. I am living proof of the power of determination and the indomitable human spirit, and I vow never to take a single moment of my life for granted.

It has been a long journey, but I'm proud of my progress over the past three years to help myself become healthier. It has taken a lot of patience, perseverance, and determination to get to where I am today. I am saying this to bring attention to myself, but we underestimate the trauma our bodies endure fighting a sickness or recovering from an illness. Three years ago, I prioritized my health and well-being; it was difficult. Too often, I think I did not choose this journey, but it chose me. We did not plan to allow COVID-19 to take so many loved ones away from us. Still, I desire to live another day, to bring about the willpower to get everyone else to see that fighting internally requires much self-encouragement.

The first year was the most challenging, as I struggled to make significant changes to my lifestyle and habits because I needed to be that one who was in a hospital fighting the effects of a pandemic illness. Still, I wanted to identify as more than a COVID survivor; I wanted to be the resilience coach who brought others to their best. I had to be patient with myself as I slowly but steadily changed my diet, exercise routine, and overall mindset. It was a constant battle to stay motivated and encouraged when I did not see immediate results. When I needed or had to walk the stairs, it was a dreaded experience to walk up and wait five minutes to catch my breath.

The second year brought visible improvements, but I still had a long way to go. My body was like time traveling, not forward, but backward, because each time I tried to feel as if I was making progress, I faced another challenge. I continued to be patient and reminded myself that progress takes time. I focused on celebrating small victories and staying consistent with my healthy habits. Sometimes, I felt frustrated and wanted to give up, but I knew I needed to keep the course and be patient.

As I entered the third year of my journey to better health, I began to see significant changes both physically and mentally. My friends even began saying living the life, which meant I was gaining good weight since the COVID experience made me lose so much of my mass that I needed to keep reminding myself that it was not a weight.

It was a gain or weight loss journey, but it was a journey of improving in all areas to ensure I could motivate someone who needed to be strong. Today, I trust that my patience and persistence finally started to pay off, and I feel more energized, stronger, and happier than ever. I realized the key to my success was staying patient and not giving up, even when going was tough.

Looking back on the past three years, I am grateful for the patience I had to muster to become healthier and allow resilience to ingrain itself in my actions. It was not easy, but it was worth it. I've learned so much about myself and what I'm capable of, and I'm excited to continue this journey toward an even healthier future.

This may be a simple basis to begin. We will explore the importance of celebrating your resilience victories. As individuals who have faced numerous challenges and obstacles, it is crucial to acknowledge and honour the strength and perseverance it took to overcome them. By celebrating your resilience victories, you boost your self-confidence and self-esteem and inspire others who may be going through similar struggles.

One powerful lesson to take away from celebrating your resilience victories is the ability to shift your mindset from one of defeat to one of triumph. Rather than dwelling on the negative aspects of your struggles, focusing on the positive outcomes and personal growth that resulted from overcoming them can be incredibly empowering. By reframing your perspective, you can see your resilience as a source of strength and resilience rather than weakness.

Another important lesson from celebrating your resilience victories is the importance of self-care and self-compassion. It is easy to neglect your well-being when faced with adversity, but taking the time to acknowledge and celebrate your accomplishments can help remind you of your worth and value. By practicing self-care and showing yourself compassion, you are better equipped to handle future challenges with grace and resilience.

Furthermore, celebrating your resilience victories can remind you of your inner strength and resilience. By reflecting on the obstacles, you have overcome and the personal growth you have experienced, you can build confidence in your ability to overcome future challenges. This newfound sense of empowerment can propel you towards even greater success and achievement in all areas of your life.

Celebrating your resilience victories is a powerful way to Honor your journey and acknowledge the strength and perseverance it took to overcome adversity. By shifting your mindset, practicing self-care, and recognizing your inner strength, you can continue to grow and thrive in the face of challenges. Remember, your resilience is not a sign of weakness but a testament to your extraordinary ability to overcome obstacles and reach success.

Maintaining Resilience in the Face of Challenges

We are bound to face challenges and obstacles that test our resilience and determination. Our true strength and character are revealed during these difficult times. Maintaining resilience in the face of challenges is crucial for overcoming adversity and reaching success. This subchapter will explore the key strategies and mindset shifts that can help you stay strong and resilient in the face of any obstacle.

> A positive mindset is one of the most important aspects of maintaining resilience. Instead of focusing on the negative aspects of a challenge, try to see it as an opportunity for growth and learning. By shifting your perspective and concentrating on the lessons that can be learned from the situation, you will be better equipped to overcome the obstacle and emerge stronger than before.

Another crucial element of maintaining resilience is developing a support system. Surround yourself with people who lift you, encourage you, and provide a listening ear when you need it most. Having a solid support system can make all the difference when facing challenges, as it reminds you that you are not alone in your struggles and that there are people who believe in your ability to overcome them.

Taking care of yourself physically, mentally, and emotionally is also important during challenging times. Make time for self-care activities that help you relax and recharge, such as exercise, meditation, or spending time in nature. Prioritizing your well-being will help you stay resilient and better equipped to face any obstacle that comes your way.

Lastly, remember that resilience is a skill that can be developed and strengthened over time. By practicing self-awareness, perseverance, and a growth mindset, you can cultivate the resilience to overcome challenges and achieve extraordinary success. Stay focused, stay positive, and never give up on yourself or your dreams. The power of resilience lies within you - embrace it and watch yourself soar to new heights of success.

Using Resilience to Navigate Change

Change is inevitable in life, but it can be challenging to navigate, whether it's a new job, a move to a different city, or a relationship shift. However, by harnessing the power of resilience, we can survive change and thrive in the face of it. Resilience is the ability to bounce back from setbacks, adapt to new circumstances, and persevere in adversity. By utilizing resilience, we can turn challenges into opportunities for growth and success.

One key aspect of using resilience to navigate change is maintaining a positive mindset. When faced with a difficult situation, getting caught up in negative thinking can be easy. However, by focusing on the potential for growth and learning that comes with change, we can shift our perspective and approach challenges optimistically. This positive mindset can help us stay motivated and resilient in uncertainty.

Another important aspect of using resilience to navigate change is practicing self-care. Change can be stressful and overwhelming, so it's crucial to care for ourselves mentally and physically during these times. This can include exercise, meditation, spending time with loved ones, or seeking support from a therapist or counsellor.

By prioritizing self-care, we can build the strength and resilience to navigate change effectively. In addition to maintaining a positive mindset and practicing self-care, it's essential to cultivate a sense of adaptability when facing change. Resilience is all about adapting to new circumstances and bouncing back from setbacks. By embracing change as an opportunity for growth and learning rather than a threat, we can develop the flexibility to navigate change with grace and resilience.

Harnessing the power of resilience can help us navigate change with confidence and grace. By maintaining a positive mindset, practicing self-care, and cultivating adaptability, we can turn challenges into opportunities for growth and success. Change may be inevitable, but we can overcome obstacles and reach our full potential with resilience as our guide. Remember, you have the strength to turn adversity into extraordinary success.

Creating a Resilient Support Network

Creating a resilient support network is vital for overcoming obstacles and reaching success. It is essential to surround yourself with positive and supportive individuals who can help uplift you during challenging times. Your support network can consist of family, friends, mentors, and even online communities. These individuals can provide encouragement, advice, and a listening ear when you need it most.

One critical component of building a resilient support network is communication. Communicating your needs and struggles with your support system is crucial. Sharing your thoughts and feelings allows others to understand better how they can support you.

Communication helps build trust and strengthen relationships within your network. Another critical aspect of creating a resilient support network is reciprocity. Just as you lean on others for support, it is essential to also offer your support to those in your network. By being a source of strength and encouragement for others, you contribute to the overall strength and resilience of the group. Remember, a strong support network is built on mutual respect and reciprocity.

To building a support network of individuals, it is also beneficial to seek out resources and tools that can help enhance your resilience. This can include books, podcasts, workshops, and online communities dedicated to personal growth and development. By continuously seeking out new knowledge and perspectives, you can strengthen your own resilience and be better equipped to handle life's challenges.

> Where creating a resilient support network is essential for overcoming obstacles and reaching success. By surrounding yourself with positive and supportive individuals, openly communicating your needs, practicing reciprocity, and seeking out additional resources, you can build a strong and resilient network that will help you navigate life's ups and downs. Remember, you are not alone in your journey – together, we can overcome any obstacle and achieve extraordinary success.

Reflecting on Your Resilience Journey

As you continue your journey of resilience, it is essential to take a moment to reflect on how far you have come. It can be easy to get caught up in the day-to-day struggles and challenges, but by taking the time to look back on your past obstacles and triumphs, you can gain a renewed sense of strength and determination. Reflecting on your resilience journey allows you to see the progress you have made and gives you the confidence to keep pushing forward.

One powerful way to reflect on your resilience journey is to journal about your experiences. Writing down your thoughts and feelings can help you process the emotions that come with overcoming adversity. Take some time each day to write about the obstacles you have faced, the lessons you have learned, and the progress you have made. By documenting your journey, you can track your growth and celebrate your victories along the way.

Another important aspect of reflecting on your resilience journey is recognizing the support systems that have helped you along the way. Whether it be friends, family, mentors, or even strangers who have offered a helping hand, acknowledging the people who have stood by your side can be incredibly empowering. Take the time to thank those who have supported you and consider how you can pay it forward by offering your support to others in need.

To look back on your past experiences, it is also essential to look forward and set goals for the future. Reflect on where you want to go next in your resilience journey and what steps you need to take to get there. By setting clear goals and creating a plan for success, you can continue to build on the resilience you have already developed and overcome even more significant challenges in the future.

In conclusion, reflecting on your resilience journey is an essential part of your growth and development. By taking the time to journal about your experiences, acknowledge your support systems, and set goals for the future, you can continue to build on your resilience and turn your adversity into extraordinary success. Remember that you can overcome any obstacle that comes your way, and by reflecting on your journey, you can harness the power of resilience to reach new heights of achievement.

Embracing Your Unique Path to Success

In life, we often find ourselves comparing our journey to success with those around us. We may feel inadequate or behind because our path looks different from others. However, it is essential to remember that success is not a one-size-fits-all journey. Each of us has our own unique path to follow, and embracing that uniqueness is critical to reaching our goals.

One of the most powerful lessons we can learn on our journey to success is to embrace our individuality. We are all unique individuals with our own strengths, weaknesses, and experiences. By recognizing and embracing what makes us different, we can leverage our strengths and navigate around our weaknesses to reach our full potential. Another important aspect of embracing our unique path to success is to let go of comparison.

It is easy to get caught up in comparing ourselves to others, but this only serves to undermine our own progress. Instead of focusing on what others are doing, we should focus on our own journey and how we can continue to grow and improve.

Embracing our unique path to success also requires us to be open to new opportunities and experiences. Success often comes when we step outside of our comfort zone and take risks. By being open to new possibilities, we can discover new passions, talents, and opportunities that can propel us towards our goals.

Ultimately, embracing our unique path to success is about being true to ourselves and following our own intuition. Trusting in our abilities and staying true to our values will ultimately lead us to our own version of success. By embracing our individuality and following our own path, we can overcome any obstacles that come our way and achieve extraordinary success.

Inspiring Others with Your Resilience Story

Do you have a story of resilience that has shaped your life? Have you overcome obstacles that seemed insurmountable at the time? Sharing your resilience story can inspire others to push through their own challenges and keep moving forward. In this subchapter, we will explore the power of sharing your resilience story and how it can impact those around you.

Your resilience story is a powerful tool that can inspire others to persevere in the face of adversity. By sharing your experiences of overcoming obstacles, you can show others that they are not alone in their struggles and that there is hope for a brighter future. Your story can serve as a beacon of light for those who are feeling lost or defeated, reminding them that they too can overcome whatever challenges they may be facing.

When you share your resilience story, you are not only inspiring others, but you are also empowering yourself. By reflecting on your past struggles and triumphs, you can gain a deeper understanding of your own strength and resilience. You may even discover new insights and lessons that can help you navigate future challenges with grace and determination. Sharing your story can be a cathartic experience that allows you to heal from past wounds and move forward with renewed purpose and clarity.

No matter your age, sharing your resilience story can have a profound impact on those around you. Whether you are a young adult just starting out on your journey or a seasoned veteran who has weathered many storms, your story can resonate with people of all ages and backgrounds.

By sharing your experiences and lessons learned, you can inspire others to tap into their own inner strength and resilience, no matter what obstacles they may face. In conclusion, sharing your resilience story is a powerful way to inspire others and empower yourself. Your story has the potential to touch the hearts of those who are struggling and show them that they too can overcome their challenges.

By sharing your experiences and the lessons you have learned along the way, you can help others see that there is always hope for a brighter future. So don't be afraid to share your story – you never know whose life you might touch with your words of wisdom and encouragement.

LESSON 2

Confronting Self Doubt

Building A Strong Foundation for Resilience

Now, I know what you're thinking - "But how can mere words have such a profound impact on my thoughts and beliefs?" Well, dear reader, let me tell you a little secret - your brain believes what you tell it. So, if you keep telling yourself that you're not good enough, guess what? Your brain will start to believe it. But if you start feeding your mind with positive, empowering words, your brain will start to believe in your limitless potential.

> *"Every day, form positive habits by taking one step at a time."*
>
> – ETHAN R. ESBACH

Self-awareness and Emotional Intelligence

In the fast-paced and ever-changing business world, business owners must cultivate self-awareness and emotional intelligence to navigate challenges and setbacks. Self-awareness is the ability to recognize and understand one's emotions, thoughts, and behaviours, while emotional intelligence is the ability to manage and control those emotions effectively. By developing these skills, business owners can better understand their strengths and weaknesses, make more informed decisions, and build stronger relationships with employees and clients.

Self-awareness is the foundation of emotional intelligence, allowing business owners to understand how their emotions and actions impact themselves and those around them. By being aware of their feelings, business owners can better regulate their responses in high-pressure situations, leading to more effective problem-solving and decision-making. Additionally, self-awareness enables business owners to identify their triggers and biases, allowing them to approach challenges with a clear and unbiased perspective.

On the other hand, emotional intelligence is the ability to recognize and manage emotions in oneself and others. This skill is essential for building strong relationships with employees, clients, and stakeholders, as it allows business owners to empathize with others, communicate effectively, and resolve conflicts constructively. Business owners can create a positive work environment that fosters collaboration, innovation, and growth by developing emotional intelligence.

To cultivate self-awareness and emotional intelligence, business owners can practice mindfulness techniques, such as meditation and journaling, to increase their awareness of their thoughts and emotions. They can also seek feedback from trusted colleagues or mentors to gain insight into their strengths and areas for improvement. By investing time and effort into developing these skills, business owners can enhance their resilience in the face of adversity and become stronger leaders in their organizations.

Overall, self-awareness and emotional intelligence are essential skills for business owners looking to overcome challenges and succeed personally and professionally. By developing these skills, business owners can build stronger relationships, make better decisions, and navigate obstacles gracefully and resiliently. Cultivating self-awareness and emotional intelligence in the competitive business world can set business owners apart and help them thrive in adversity.

Developing a Growth Mindset

To thrive in the fast-paced and ever-changing world of business, business owners must develop a growth mindset. A growth mindset is the belief that one's abilities and intelligence can be developed through hard work, dedication, and perseverance. This mindset enables individuals to embrace challenges, learn from failures, and continuously improve themselves.

One key component of developing a growth mindset is embracing challenges as opportunities for growth and learning. Instead of shying away from complex tasks or situations, business owners with a growth mindset see them as a chance to stretch their abilities and improve their skills. They can achieve personal growth and development by facing challenges head-on and pushing themselves out of their comfort zones.

Another critical aspect of developing a growth mindset is viewing failures as learning experiences. Instead of seeing setbacks as the end of the road, business owners with a growth mindset see them as valuable opportunities to learn, grow, and improve. They can bounce back more robustly and resiliently by analysing their failures, identifying what went wrong, and adjusting for the future.

Developing a growth mindset involves seeking feedback and constructive criticism from others. Business owners with a growth mindset understand that feedback is a valuable tool for personal growth and development. By listening to others' perspectives, learning from their insights, and adjusting accordingly, they can continuously improve themselves and their businesses.

Developing a growth mindset is essential for business owners who want to thrive in today's competitive business environment. By embracing challenges, learning from failures, seeking feedback, and continuously striving for personal growth and development, business owners can cultivate a resilient mindset that will enable them to overcome challenges and succeed in their businesses.

Building a Support Network

Building a Support Network is crucial for business owners looking to develop a resilient mindset when facing challenges. The entrepreneurship journey can sometimes be lonely and overwhelming, so having a solid support system is essential. Your support network can consist of friends, family, mentors, and like-minded individuals who understand the unique challenges of running a business. These individuals can provide you with guidance, encouragement, and a different perspective when you need it most.

One of the first steps in building a support network is identifying the people in your life who can offer you support. This may include family members who believe in your vision, friends willing to lend a listening ear, or mentors with industry experience. It's essential to surround yourself with people who uplift you and inspire you to keep pushing forward, even when faced with obstacles. Building relationships with these individuals takes time and effort, but the benefits of having a solid support network are invaluable.

Networking events, industry conferences, and online communities are great places to connect with like-minded individuals who can become part of your support network. These platforms provide opportunities to meet new people, exchange ideas, and build relationships with others who share your passion for personal growth and development. By actively participating in these events and communities, you can expand your support network and gain valuable insights from others who have faced similar challenges in their businesses.

In addition to seeking support from others, offering support to those in your network is essential. Building a solid support system is a two-way street; you can strengthen your relationships with them by being there for others in their times of need. By fostering a culture of support and collaboration within your network, you can create a positive and empowering environment where everyone can thrive and grow together.

By building a support network is critical to developing a resilient mindset as a business owner. Surrounding yourself with individuals who believe in you, offer guidance, and inspire you to keep pushing forward can make all the difference in your ability to overcome challenges and achieve success.

By actively seeking out and nurturing these relationships, you can create a strong foundation of support that will sustain you through the ups and downs of entrepreneurship. Remember, you don't have to go it alone – with a strong support network, you can face any challenge with confidence and resilience.

Understanding Negative Self-Talk - The Power of Words

Welcome to the subchapter on "The Power of Words" in our guide to overcoming negative self-talk! As adults, we often underestimate the impact that our words can have on our own thoughts and beliefs. But fear not, dear reader, for I am here to show you just how powerful words can be in silencing that pesky inner critic.

Imagine your inner critic as a tiny, annoying little gremlin perched on your shoulder, constantly whispering negative thoughts in your ear. Now, imagine that you have a secret weapon to shut that gremlin up - positive affirmations! By choosing your words carefully and repeating uplifting phrases to yourself, you can send that inner critic running for the hills.

But beware, dear reader, for the power of words works both ways. Just as positive affirmations can lift you up, negative self-talk can drag you down faster than a lead balloon. So, be mindful of the words you choose to speak to yourself. Remember, you are your own worst critic, so why not become your own best cheerleader instead?

> Now, I know what you're thinking - "But how can mere words have such a profound impact on my thoughts and beliefs?" Well, dear reader, let me tell you a little secret - your brain believes what you tell it. So, if you

keep telling yourself that you're not good enough, guess what? Your brain will start to believe it. But if you start feeding your mind with positive, empowering words, your brain will start to believe in your limitless potential.

I say to you never underestimate the power of words in shaping your thoughts and beliefs. Use positive affirmations to drown out that inner critic and watch as your self-limiting beliefs crumble before your eyes. Remember, you have the power to silence that pesky gremlin once and for all - all it takes is a few well-chosen words and a whole lot of self-love.

Recognizing Patterns of Negative Self-Talk

Congratulations, you've made it to the chapter where we get to dive deep into the wild world of negative self-talk. But fear not, my fellow adults, for we are armed with the tools to silence that pesky inner critic once and for all. First things first, let's talk about recognizing those sneaky patterns of negative self-talk that like to creep up on us when we least expect it.

Picture this: you're going about your day, minding your own business, when suddenly you hear a voice in your head saying, "You're not good enough" or "You'll never succeed." Sound familiar? That, my friends, is the sound of negative self-talk rearing its ugly head. But fear not, for now that you're aware of these patterns, you can start to spot them and shut them down like a boss.

One common pattern of negative self-talk is the all-or-nothing mindset. You know, the one where you think you must be perfect or it's not worth even trying. But let me tell you a little secret: perfection is overrated. Embrace your flaws, embrace your imperfections, and watch as that inner critic starts to lose its power over you.

Another pattern to look out for is catastrophizing. This is when you blow things way out of proportion and imagine the worst possible outcome. But let me ask you this: how many times has the worst-case scenario come true? Probably not as often as your inner critic would have you believe. So next time you catch yourself catastrophizing, take a step back, take a deep breath, and remind yourself that things are rarely as bad as they seem.

Through recognizing patterns of negative self-talk is the first step towards silencing that inner critic once and for all. So, keep an eye out for those sneaky patterns, challenge them with a healthy dose of humour, and watch as your self-limiting beliefs start to lose their grip on you. Remember, you are in control of your thoughts, not the other way around. Now go forth, my fellow adults, and conquer that negative self-talk like the fierce warriors you are!

How Negative Self-Talk Affects Your Well-being

Have you ever caught yourself in a heated argument with the little voice in your head? You know, the one that constantly tells you that you're not good enough, smart enough, or capable enough? Well, that voice is what we like to call the "inner critic," and it can wreak havoc on your well-being if you let it. Negative self-talk can have a profound impact on your mental and emotional health.

When you constantly berate yourself with thoughts like "I'm such a failure" or "I'll never succeed," you start to believe these lies as truth. This can lead to feelings of low self-esteem, anxiety, and depression. So, if you want to improve your well-being, it's time to silence that inner critic once and for all. One-way negative self-talk affects your well-being is by creating self-limiting beliefs.

When you constantly tell yourself that you're not good enough, you start to believe it. This can prevent you from taking risks, pursuing your goals, or even trying new things. In other words, your inner critic becomes the gatekeeper to your success, holding you back from reaching your full potential.

Another way negative self-talk affects your well-being is by draining your energy and motivation. When you're constantly bombarded with thoughts of self-doubt and criticism, it's hard to muster up the energy to tackle your daily tasks or work towards your goals. It's like having a negative Nancy constantly whispering in your ear, sapping your enthusiasm and drive.

But fear not, dear reader, for there is hope! By learning to recognize and challenge your negative self-talk, you can take back control of your inner dialogue and boost your well-being. So, the next time your inner critic pipes up with a snarky remark, tell it to take a hike and replace it with a more positive and empowering thought. Remember, you oversee your thoughts, not the other way around. So, go ahead and silence that inner critic once and for all. Your well-being will thank you!

LESSON 3

Its Technically Technical Strategies

Strategies for Overcoming Adversity

In the face of uncertainty, it is also important to cultivate a sense of adaptability and flexibility. Business owners who are willing to pivot and adjust their strategies in response to changing circumstances are more likely to thrive in a rapidly evolving marketplace. By remaining agile and open to new possibilities, we can turn uncertainty into an opportunity for growth and innovation.

> *"Take action that will make your future self-proud."*
>
> – ETHAN R. ESBACH

Cognitive Restructuring Techniques

In the world of business, challenges and setbacks are inevitable. As business owners, it is crucial to develop a resilient mindset to overcome these obstacles and continue moving forward towards success. Cognitive restructuring techniques are one powerful tool that can help build this resilience.

Cognitive restructuring involves identifying and changing negative thought patterns that may be holding you back. By challenging and reframing these thoughts, you can shift your mindset towards a more positive and adaptive outlook. This can help you to better cope with stress, setbacks, and uncertainties in the business world.

One effective cognitive restructuring technique is called cognitive reframing. This involves looking at a situation from a different perspective to change your emotional response to it. For example, instead of viewing a failed business venture as a personal failure, you can reframe it as a learning experience that will help you grow and improve in the future.

Another technique is called cognitive distancing, which involves stepping back from a situation and viewing it from a more objective standpoint. This can help you to see things more clearly and rationally rather than being overwhelmed by emotions or biases. I know this one can be a bit of a challenge since we all are passionate about our ambitions towards a viewpoint, but synergy is understanding your point from the view of someone else's understanding and reaching a consensus. By practicing cognitive distancing, you can make more informed decisions and respond more effectively to challenges.

Practicing cognitive flexibility is the key to developing a resilient mindset. This involves being open to different viewpoints and being willing to adapt your thinking in response to new information or circumstances. Over many years, we have become rigid in our thinking and overly committed to a self-developed outcome, which disallows our lives to grow in areas we lack either wisdom or knowledge.

I have needed to work on being flexible in my thinking, and I encourage you too to see how working with a synergy mindset can help you better navigate the ever-changing landscape of the business world and bounce back from setbacks more easily. Overall, incorporating cognitive restructuring techniques into your daily routine can help you build resilience in the face of challenges and uncertainties. By challenging negative thought patterns, reframing situations in a more positive light, and practicing cognitive flexibility, you can develop a resilient mindset that will serve you well in both your personal growth and business success.

Embracing Change and Uncertainty

Embracing change and uncertainty is a crucial aspect of developing a resilient mindset in both business and personal growth. As business owners, it is essential to understand that change is inevitable and learning to adapt to uncertainty is key to long-term success. By embracing change, we allow ourselves to remain flexible and open to new opportunities that may arise.

Opportunities that shape you for more challenging moments but in respect of overall growth. One can only say that an opportunity that is difficult and has been overcome is more rewarding than an opportunity that comes with ease. Think about you fighting harder for something to win and make it, as opposed to someone fighting on your behalf and allowing you to benefit from it.

One of the first steps in embracing change and uncertainty is to shift our mindset from one of fear and resistance to one of acceptance and curiosity. Instead of viewing change as a threat, we can see it as a chance for growth and innovation. By reframing our perspective, we can approach uncertain situations with a sense of excitement and possibility, rather than dread or anxiety.

I remember when trying to control the outcome with fear made the outcome become more negative than if I were to view it as what happens will allow me to grow in each of the positive or negative outcomes. Now a resilient person would not prepare overly well for an outcome but rather be ready when an outcome presents itself.

Another important aspect of embracing change is building resilience through self-care and self-awareness. Taking care of our physical and mental well-being allows us to better cope with the challenges that come with uncertainty. By practicing mindfulness and self-reflection, we can develop a deeper understanding of our own strengths and weaknesses, enabling us to navigate change with more confidence and grace.

> In the face of uncertainty, it is also important to cultivate a sense of adaptability and flexibility. Business owners who are willing to pivot and adjust their strategies in response to changing circumstances are more likely to thrive in a rapidly evolving marketplace. By remaining agile and open to new possibilities, we can turn uncertainty into an opportunity for growth and innovation.

Ultimately, embracing change and uncertainty is a mindset that can be developed over time with practice and dedication. By cultivating resilience, self-awareness, and adaptability, business owners can position themselves for success in the face of any challenge that comes their way. By approaching change with a positive and proactive attitude, we can harness its transformative power to propel our businesses and personal growth to new heights.

Practicing Mindfulness and Stress Management

In the competitive world of business, stress is often an unavoidable reality. As business owners, it is crucial to develop strategies for managing stress and practicing mindfulness to maintain a resilient mindset. By incorporating these practices into your daily routine, you can improve your overall well-being and enhance your ability to overcome challenges in your personal and professional life.

Mindfulness is the practice of being present in the moment, without judgment or distraction. By focusing on the present moment, you can reduce stress and increase your ability to make clear, rational decisions. Incorporating mindfulness techniques such as deep breathing, and meditation, into your daily routine can help you stay grounded and focused, even in the face of difficult situations.

Stress management is another key aspect of maintaining a resilient mindset. By identifying your triggers and developing healthy coping mechanisms, you can effectively manage stress and prevent it from overwhelming you. Techniques such as exercise, proper nutrition, and setting boundaries can help you reduce stress levels and improve your overall well-being.

One effective strategy for practicing mindfulness and managing stress is to incorporate regular breaks into your workday. Taking short breaks to engage in mindfulness exercises or physical activity can help you recharge and refocus, leading to increased productivity and creativity.

Additionally, setting boundaries around work hours and creating a work-life balance can help you prevent burnout and maintain your resilience in the face of challenges. A foggy mind become irrational in thinking which at times leads to actions that thinking back when the mind resets amount to regret and more.

To practice mindfulness and stress management is essential for business owners looking to cultivate a resilient mindset. By incorporating these practices into your daily routine, you can improve your ability to navigate challenges and setbacks with grace and determination. By taking care of your mental and emotional well-being, you can position yourself for success in both your personal growth and development and your business endeavours.

Recognizing Your Health Challenges

Recognizing your health challenges is the first step towards overcoming them. It is important to acknowledge and accept the obstacles that you are facing to begin the healing process. Whether you are dealing with a chronic illness, injury, or mental health issue, understanding and accepting your situation is crucial for moving forward. By recognizing your health challenges, you are taking control of your own well-being and empowering yourself to make positive changes.

One of the most powerful lessons that can be learned from facing health challenges is resilience. Resilience is the ability to bounce back from adversity and overcome obstacles with strength and determination. When you recognize your health challenges, you are given the opportunity to develop and strengthen your resilience. By facing your challenges head-on and refusing to give up, you can turn your adversity into extraordinary success. Resilience is a key trait that can help you navigate through difficult times and emerge stronger on the other side.

> Inspirational guidance can be invaluable for individuals facing health challenges. Hearing stories of others who have overcome similar obstacles can provide hope and motivation during difficult times. By learning from those who have faced adversity and come out on top, you can gain valuable insights and strategies for overcoming your own health challenges. Inspirational guidance can help you see that you are not alone in your struggles and that there is a way forward towards healing and recovery. A journey I never planned but was it rewarding. Recovering from a coma in 2021 and learning to do the basics again needed me to rediscover myself first because the person I needed to be to see my situation as stepping forward into purpose rather than misfortune needed me to understand who I am developing becoming which is resilient!

From ages 18 to 90, individuals face a wide range of health challenges. Whether you are a young adult struggling with a mental health issue or an older adult dealing with a chronic illness, recognizing your health challenges is the first step towards healing.

By acknowledging your obstacles and seeking out support and guidance, you can begin the journey towards better health and well-being. Remember that you are not defined by your health challenges, but rather by how you choose to face and overcome them.

Recognizing your health challenges is a crucial step towards healing and recovery. By acknowledging and accepting your obstacles, you are taking control of your own well-being and empowering yourself to make positive changes. Through resilience, inspirational guidance, and a determination to overcome adversity, you can turn your health challenges into opportunities for growth and success. No matter your age or the nature of your health challenges, remember that you are not alone and that there is always hope for a brighter future ahead. Look at me? Stay focussed! You will win!

In life, we are often faced with unexpected health challenges that force us to confront our own mortality and limitations. Whether it's a sudden diagnosis, chronic illness, or physical injury, accepting our reality is the first step towards healing from within. It's natural to feel anger, fear, and sadness when confronted with a health challenge; I remember waking up from my coma thinking why does this feel so difficult? Why me? why do I need to endure? But it's important to remember that these emotions are a normal part of the healing process. By acknowledging and accepting our reality, we can begin to move forward with grace and resilience.

One of the most powerful lessons we can learn from facing a health challenge is that we are stronger and more resilient than we ever thought possible. In the face of adversity, we discover a newfound sense of inner strength and courage that carries us through even the toughest of times. By accepting our reality and embracing our challenges, we can tap into this inner power and use it to propel us towards extraordinary success.

When we accept our reality, we free ourselves from the burden of denial and resistance. Instead of wasting energy fighting against our circumstances, we can redirect our focus towards finding solutions and creating positive change in our lives. Acceptance allows us to let go of the past and embrace the present moment with gratitude and mindfulness. By accepting our reality, we open ourselves up to new possibilities and opportunities for growth and healing.

Inspirational guidance is essential for individuals facing health challenges, as it provides a source of hope, motivation, and encouragement during difficult times. By sharing stories of resilience and triumph, we can inspire others to embrace their reality and find the strength within themselves to overcome any obstacle.

Through the power of inspirational guidance, we can transform our health challenges into opportunities for personal growth and transformation. Ultimately, accepting our reality is a powerful act of self-love and self-compassion. By acknowledging our struggles and vulnerabilities, we pave the way for healing and transformation to take place.

No matter what health challenges we may face, we can find solace in the knowledge that we are not alone in our journey. By accepting our reality and embracing our challenges, we can turn adversity into extraordinary success and emerge stronger, wiser, and more resilient than ever before.

Finding Strength in Vulnerability

In our journey to healing, it is vital to recognize the power in vulnerability. Many of us have been conditioned to believe that showing vulnerability is a sign of weakness, but it takes great strength to open about our struggles and pain. By allowing ourselves to be vulnerable, we create space for healing and growth.

When we embrace our vulnerability, we give ourselves permission to fully experience our emotions and confront our fears. This willingness to be open and honest with us and others can lead to profound healing and transformation. Through vulnerability, we can connect with others on a deeper level and build supportive relationships that can help us navigate our health challenges.

It is important to remember that vulnerability is not a sign of defeat but rather a sign of courage and resilience. By allowing ourselves to be vulnerable, we can tap into our inner strength and find the courage to face our health challenges head-on. It is only by being willing to confront our vulnerabilities that we can truly begin the healing process and move toward a place of greater health and well-being. As we navigate our health challenges, it is important to remember that vulnerability is not a sign of weakness, but rather a source of strength. By embracing our vulnerabilities and allowing ourselves to be open and honest about our struggles, we can find the inner strength to overcome even the toughest of obstacles. It is through vulnerability that we can tap into our resilience and find the power within ourselves to turn our adversity into extraordinary success.

I believe strength in vulnerability is a powerful tool for healing and growth. We can tap into our inner strength and resilience by embracing our vulnerabilities and allowing ourselves to be open and honest about our struggles. It is through vulnerability that we can find the courage to face our health challenges head-on and turn our adversity into extraordinary success. Remember, vulnerability is not a sign of weakness, but a sign of courage and resilience. Embrace your vulnerabilities and find the strength within to overcome any obstacle that comes your way.

Exploring the Mind-Body Connection

Delving into the fascinating world of the mind-body connection and how it can play a crucial role in overcoming health challenges. The mind-body connection links our thoughts, emotions, beliefs, and physical health. Research has shown that our mental and emotional state can profoundly impact our physical well-being and vice versa. By understanding and harnessing this connection, we can empower ourselves to take control of our health and well-being.

One powerful lesson we can learn from exploring the mind-body connection is the importance of cultivating a positive mindset. Studies have shown that individuals who maintain a positive attitude and outlook on life tend to experience better health outcomes and faster recovery from illness. By focusing on the positive aspects of our lives and practicing gratitude, we can boost our immune system, reduce stress levels, and improve our overall well-being. This resilient mindset can help us navigate health challenges with grace and strength.

Another key aspect of the mind-body connection is the impact of stress on our health. Chronic stress has been linked to a wide range of health issues, including heart disease, digestive problems, and immune system dysfunction. By learning how to manage stress through techniques such as mindfulness, meditation, and deep breathing exercises, we can protect our physical health and promote healing from within. Taking care of our mental and emotional well-being is just as important as taking care of our physical health when it comes to overcoming health challenges.

For individuals facing health challenges, the mind-body connection can provide a source of inspiration and guidance. By tapping into our inner resilience and strength, we can turn adversity into extraordinary success. Through practices such as visualization, positive affirmations, and self-care, we can harness the power of our thoughts and emotions to support our healing journey. By cultivating a sense of empowerment and self-belief, we can overcome obstacles and achieve optimal health and well-being.

Easy said than done but exploring the mind-body connection can offer invaluable insights and tools for individuals facing health challenges. By embracing the power of our thoughts, emotions, and beliefs, we can transform our adversity into extraordinary success. Through practices that promote a positive mindset, stress management, and self-care, we can tap into our inner resilience and strength. By taking a holistic approach to healing from within, we can empower ourselves to overcome health challenges and thrive at any age.

Developing a Positive Mindset

So much has been said about mindset and having resilience in the mind but how? Let's explore the importance of developing a positive mindset when facing health challenges. It is important to understand that our thoughts and beliefs have a powerful impact on our physical and emotional well-being. By cultivating a positive mindset, we can better cope with adversity and improve our overall health.

> One of the first steps in developing a positive mindset is to practice gratitude. Take time each day to reflect on the things you are grateful for, no matter how small they may seem. This simple practice can help shift your focus from what is going wrong to what is going right in your life, leading to a more positive outlook.

Another important aspect of developing a positive mindset is challenging negative thoughts and beliefs. When faced with a health challenge, it is easy to become overwhelmed with fear and doubt. By recognizing and reframing negative thoughts, you can begin to see your situation form a more hopeful and empowering perspective.

It is also important to surround yourself with positivity. Seek out supportive and uplifting individuals who can provide encouragement and inspiration during difficult times. Engage in activities that bring you joy and relaxation, such as spending time in nature, practicing mindfulness, or pursuing creative hobbies. By taking these steps to develop a positive mindset, you can transform your adversity into an opportunity for growth and resilience. Remember that you have the power to overcome any health challenge with grace and strength. Stay focused on the present moment, stay connected to your inner strength, and believe in your ability to heal from within.

Seeking Support from Others

In times of adversity and health challenges, seeking support from others can make a world of difference in your healing journey. It can be difficult to navigate through tough times alone, which is why reaching out for help is crucial for your emotional and physical well-being.

During my COVID-19 journey, I remember there was no hospital visitation allowed; I only had my mind to occupy myself, and the hospital staff who did an outstanding work on nursing me back to health. Where would life have navigated itself if I were to see being alone as a hostile place to be? I used the unfortunate situation and the silence in normal life to become more aware of the finer things in life, like being able to think, breathe, and even, at some point, appreciate using the body for activities we do on autopilot.

In moments of vulnerability, I recognized the immense value of support from friends, family, support groups, and professionals. Despite not having the physical presence of my loved ones, I realized the incredible strength and encouragement a solid support system provides.

I truly appreciate the unwavering support I have received, understanding that circumstances may have limited their ability to provide physical assistance. One of the most powerful lessons you can learn from seeking support from others is the importance of vulnerability.

It takes courage to open about your struggles and ask for help, but doing so can lead to deeper connections and understanding with those around you. By allowing yourself to be vulnerable, you are giving others the opportunity to support and uplift you in your time of need.

Another important aspect of seeking support from others is the validation and empathy you receive. When you share your experiences with others, you may find that they can relate to what you're going through and offer words of comfort and understanding. Knowing that you're not alone in your struggles can be incredibly comforting and can help you feel less isolated in your journey towards healing.

There is great power in having emotional support, seeking help from others can also provide you with practical guidance and resources to aid in your healing process. Whether it's advice on treatment options, recommendations for healthcare providers, or tips for managing symptoms, the support you receive from others can help you make informed decisions about your health and well-being.

Overall, seeking support from others is a powerful tool for overcoming health challenges and turning adversity into extraordinary success. By reaching out to those around you, you can build a strong network of support that will help you navigate through difficult times with resilience and strength. Remember, you don't have to face your health challenges alone – there are people who care about you and want to help you on your healing journey.

Setting Realistic Goals

Setting realistic goals is a crucial step in overcoming health challenges and achieving success. It is important for individuals of all ages, from 18 to 90, to understand the importance of setting achievable goals that align with their current circumstances and abilities. Not just in this age gap but I am trying to drive a point more than speak to a certain group of individuals.

By setting realistic goals, individuals can establish a clear path towards healing and recovery, while also maintaining a positive mindset throughout the journey. When setting goals, it is essential to consider your current health condition and limitations. It is important to be honest with yourself about what you can realistically achieve given your circumstances. Setting goals that are too ambitious or unrealistic can lead to feelings of failure and frustration, which can hinder progress towards healing.

By setting these realistic goals that are attainable, individuals can maintain a sense of motivation and accomplishment as they work towards overcoming their health challenges. In addition to considering your current health condition, it is important to set specific, measurable, achievable, relevant, and time-bound goals (SMART). By following the SMART criteria, individuals can create clear and actionable goals, making it easier to track progress and stay focused on the end goal. Setting SMART goals can help individuals stay on track and motivated throughout their healing journey, ultimately leading to greater success in overcoming health challenges.

It is also important for individuals facing health challenges to seek support and guidance from healthcare professionals, friends, and family members when setting goals. Consulting with healthcare providers can help individuals establish realistic goals based on their medical condition and treatment plan. Additionally, having the support of loved ones can provide encouragement and accountability as individuals work towards achieving their goals.

By involving others in the goal-setting process, individuals can increase their chances of success and maintain a positive outlook on their healing journey. We all are guilty of the fact but setting realistic goals is a vital step in overcoming health challenges and achieving success. By considering your current health condition, following the SMART criteria, and seeking support from healthcare providers and loved ones, individuals can establish achievable goals that align with their abilities and circumstances. Setting realistic goals can help individuals maintain motivation, track progress, and ultimately lead to greater success in overcoming health challenges. Remember, healing is a journey, and by setting realistic goals, individuals can turn their adversity into extraordinary success.

Creating a Holistic Treatment Plan

Creating a holistic treatment plan for individuals facing health challenges of any kind comes at a price but it is very important. By addressing all aspects of your well-being – physical, mental, emotional, and spiritual – you can truly heal from within and overcome obstacles that may seem insurmountable. A few key components of a holistic treatment plan I will be mentioning and how you can tailor it to your unique needs and preferences.

The first step in creating a holistic treatment plan is to assess your current health status and identify areas that need improvement. This may involve consulting with healthcare professionals, such as doctors, therapists, and nutritionists, to get a comprehensive understanding of your condition. Once you have a clear picture of your health, you can begin to set goals and establish a roadmap for achieving them.

Traditional medical interventions and a holistic treatment plan may also include alternative therapies such as acupuncture, massage, yoga, and meditation. These practices can help to reduce stress, improve circulation, and promote overall well-being. By incorporating a variety of modalities into your treatment plan, you can address both the physical and emotional aspects of your health challenges.

We often underestimate the important aspect of a holistic treatment plan: nutrition. Eating a balanced diet rich in fruits, vegetables, whole grains, and lean proteins can provide your body with the nutrients it needs to heal and function optimally. Additionally, avoiding processed foods, sugary drinks, and excessive alcohol can help reduce inflammation and support your body's natural healing processes. How often do we say we are going to begin but find ourselves still at the start of beginning.

Finally, a holistic treatment plan should also include self-care practices that promote mental and emotional well-being. This may involve setting aside time for relaxation, engaging in hobbies that bring you joy, and connecting with supportive friends and family members.

I have found this is important since seeing the benefits of being well rounded and not only career driven can be more rewarding than placing health at risk for the purpose of draining ventures. By nourishing your mind and spirit, you can cultivate resilience and inner strength to face any health challenge that comes your way. Remember, healing from within is a journey, and by taking a holistic approach, you can empower yourself to overcome adversity and achieve extraordinary success.

Making Self-Care a Priority

In today's fast-paced world, it can be easy to neglect our own well-being in favour of meeting the demands of work, family, and other responsibilities. However, making self-care a priority is essential for maintaining good health and overall well-being. By taking the time to care for us, we not only improve our physical health but also our mental and emotional health.

One of the first steps in making self-care a priority is recognizing the importance of putting yourself first. Many of us are conditioned to put others' needs ahead of our own, but it is crucial to remember that we cannot pour from an empty cup. By taking care of ourselves first, we are better able to care for others and handle the challenges that life may throw our way. Self-care looks different for everyone, so it is important to find what works best for you. This could include activities such as exercise, meditation, spending time with loved ones, or engaging in hobbies that bring you joy. The key is to prioritize activities that help you relax, recharge, and rejuvenate your mind, body, and spirit.

It is also important to set boundaries and learn to say no when necessary. Taking on too many commitments can lead to burnout and can have a negative impact on your health. By setting boundaries and only taking on what you can handle, you can better prioritize your self-care and avoid spreading yourself too thin.

Making self-care a priority is essential for overcoming health challenges and maintaining overall well-being. By recognizing the importance of putting yourself first, finding activities that bring you joy and relaxation, and setting boundaries to protect your own well-being, you can create a healthier and happier life.

Remember, you deserve to care for yourself just as much as you care for others. One of the goals I have always wanted to achieve is to become an Ironman. So, as I began on my journey to doing endurance sports, I realized that it is not as easy to become endurance ready. We look at the athletes doing the comrades falling to their knees at the finish line.

Going through training prepares you, but what else does a person need to have resilience in a sport? What are the tools required? I found that mental toughness is not only about the mind but what the mind tells the body and what the body wants to believe. Either your body listens to your mind or your body hits snooze, we all know snoozy suzzy? Comes mostly in winter but to some all year round but...

Let's understand how to overcome suzzy by working on the mindset in sport, toughness.

The Importance of Mental Toughness in Endurance Sports

Mental toughness is a crucial part of success in endurance sports, especially in the grueling world of Ironman competitions. The ability to push through pain, fatigue, and doubt is what sets champions apart from the rest. In the face of adversity, it is mental strength that will carry you through to the finish line. It is not just about physical strength, but about the resilience of the mind to overcome any obstacle that comes your way.

> Endurance athletes must cultivate mental toughness through consistent training and mental preparation. Visualization techniques, positive self-talk, and goal setting are all tools that can help build mental resilience. By visualizing yourself crossing the finish line, repeating affirmations of strength and determination, and setting specific, achievable goals, you can train your mind to stay focused and positive during the toughest moments of your race.

In the heat of competition, mental toughness can be the difference between giving up and pushing through to achieve your goals. It is in those moments of doubt and fatigue that mental strength truly shines. By staying present in the moment, focusing on your breathing, and reminding yourself of your training and preparation, you can overcome any challenge that comes your way.

The mental fortitude needed to complete an Ironman race is unlike any other. It is a test of your physical and mental limits, pushing you to your breaking point and beyond. But with the right mental strategies in place, you can conquer any obstacle that stands in your way. By believing in yourself, staying focused on your goals, and supporting a positive mindset, you can achieve greatness in the world of endurance sports.

Remember, mental toughness is not something you are born with – it is something that you must cultivate and nurture through consistent practice and dedication. By developing your mental strength, you can become a true Ironman warrior, capable of overcoming any challenge that comes your way. So, train your mind as hard as you train your body, and watch as your mental toughness propels you to new heights of success in endurance sports.

Breaking Down Mental Barriers in Ironman Training

When it comes to Ironman training, the physical demands are only half the battle. The mental hurdles that athletes face can often be the biggest challenge to overcome. To succeed in this grueling endurance event, it is essential to break down the mental barriers that may be holding you back. By developing a strong mindset and mental resilience, you can push through the toughest moments of training and race day. I remember races run, sports events entered for and competing, it's all about how you manage to speak to your breaking point with a winning mindset.

One of the first steps in breaking down mental barriers in Ironman training is to show and acknowledge your fears and doubts. It is normal to have moments of uncertainty and anxiety when facing such a daunting challenge. However, it is important to confront these thoughts head-on and work through them.

By shining a light on your fears, you can begin to understand their root causes and develop strategies to overcome them. I remember starting and ending training programs, I remember trying training programs, and one thing I have come to realize is that you can begin, but without knowing the reasons why and understanding the purpose in setting goals, breaking points will arrive, and failure will come stacking like bricks.

Another key aspect of overcoming mental barriers in Ironman training is to cultivate a positive and resilient mindset. Instead of dwelling on negative thoughts or setbacks, focus on the progress you have made and the strengths you own. Visualize yourself crossing the finish line and achieving your goals, no matter how challenging they may seem. By adopting a mindset of positivity and resilience, you can build the mental fortitude needed to tackle the toughest moments of training and racing.

Not only a positive mindset, but mental preparation for your Ironman also involves setting realistic goals and expectations. It is important to set up clear and achievable aims for your training and race day performance. By breaking down your goals into smaller, manageable steps, you can track your progress and stay motivated throughout the training process. Remember that progress is not always linear, and setbacks are a natural part of the journey. Stay focused on your long-term goals and trust in your training and preparation.

Ultimately, breaking down mental barriers in Ironman training requires dedication, perseverance, and a willingness to push beyond your comfort zone. By developing a strong mindset, cultivating positivity and resilience, and setting realistic goals, you can overcome the mental hurdles that may be holding you back. Remember that you can achieve greatness, and that the only limits that exist are the ones you place on yourself. Embrace the challenge, trust in your abilities, and let your inner Ironman warrior shine through.

Developing a Positive Mindset for Race Day Success

Are you an endurance athlete gearing up for an Ironman race? Do you want to ensure that you are mentally prepared for the challenges that lie ahead on race day? Developing a positive mindset is crucial for achieving success in any athletic endeavor, and Ironman is no exception. During my research into what an Ironman race day plan looks like I stumbled upon key strategies to help you cultivate a positive mindset that will propel you towards victory on race day.

The first step in developing a positive mindset for race day success is to visualize yourself achieving your goals. Take some time each day to imagine crossing the finish line, feeling strong and triumphant. Visualizing success can help build confidence and mental resilience, making it easier to push through the tough moments during the race. By focusing on your desired outcome and believing in your ability to achieve it, you are setting yourself up for success.

Another important aspect of developing a positive mindset for race day success is to practice positive self-talk. Be mindful of the thoughts that enter your mind and make a conscious effort to replace any negative self-talk with positive affirmations. Remind yourself of your strength, determination, and resilience. By cultivating a positive internal dialogue, you can boost your self-confidence and mental fortitude, helping you stay focused and motivated during the race.

Remember visualization and positive self-talk from chapters before, it is essential to stay present and focused on the task at hand during the race. Avoid getting caught up in negative thoughts or worrying about things beyond your control. Instead, concentrate on each moment, each step, each breath. By staying present and focusing on the present moment, you can overcome challenges more effectively and perform at your best.

Lastly, surround yourself with positivity and support on race day. Seek out friends, family, coaches, and fellow athletes who believe in you and your abilities. Their encouragement and positive energy can help lift you up when you are feeling down or struggling during the race.

Remember, a positive mindset is contagious, so by surrounding yourself with positivity, you can boost your own mental strength and resilience. With the right mindset and mental preparation, you can conquer the Ironman race and achieve your goals. Believe in yourself, stay positive, and embrace the challenges that lie ahead. You are a warrior, and you have what it takes to succeed. Go out there and show the world what you are made of! Easier said than done? Let me help you build the resilience you need. Although I right this book with the ironman goal in mind to complete, I am writing from the basis of principles, discipline and concepts that focus on how to implement.

Establishing Clear and Achievable Goals for Your Ironman Journey

To succeed in your Ironman journey, it is essential to prove clear and achievable goals that will guide you towards achieving your ultimate dream of crossing that finish line. Setting goals that are specific, measurable, attainable, relevant, and time-bound (SMART) will help you stay focused and motivated throughout your training and race day. By clearly defining what you want to achieve, you can create a roadmap that will lead you to success.

When setting your goals for your Ironman journey, it is important to dream big but also be realistic about what you can conduct. While it is important to challenge yourself and push beyond your limits, it is equally important to set goals that are within your reach. By setting achievable goals, you will build confidence in your abilities and stay motivated to continue pushing yourself towards success. Again, sounds easy. Not at all, it requires the person who sees the value in becoming the ultimate best as possible not probable.

> Visualizing your goals and imagining yourself crossing the finish line can be a powerful tool in helping you stay motivated and focused on your journey. By creating a mental image of your success and holding onto that vision throughout your training, you will be able to overcome any obstacles that come your way and stay committed to achieving your goals. Remember, the mind is a powerful tool and by harnessing its power, you can achieve anything you set your mind to.

One cannot only focus on setting clear and achievable goals, it is important to break down your goals into smaller, manageable milestones that will help you track your progress and stay on course. By setting short-term goals that lead you towards your goal of completing an Ironman, you will be able to celebrate your successes along the way and stay motivated to keep pushing forward. Remember, each step you take brings you closer to your dream, so stay focused and keep moving forward towards your goals.

Working to clear and achievable goals for your Ironman journey is essential for success. By setting SMART goals, dreaming big, visualizing success, and breaking down your goals into manageable milestones, you can stay focused, motivated, and committed to achieving your ultimate dream of crossing that finish line. Remember, the journey may be tough, but with a sharp vision and unwavering determination, you can conquer any challenge that comes your way. Believe in yourself, stay focused, and keep pushing forward towards your goals. You can achieve greatness, so go out there and make your Ironman dream a reality.

Utilizing Visualization Techniques to Enhance Performance

Visualization techniques are a powerful tool that can help enhance your performance as an endurance athlete, especially when preparing for an Ironman race. By incorporating visualization into your training routine, you can mentally prepare yourself for the challenges ahead and improve your overall focus and confidence.

One of the key benefits of visualization is that it allows you to mentally rehearse the race in your mind, helping you familiarize yourself with the course and visualize yourself crossing the finish line successfully. These techniques I have implemented into my sports on a normal basic training platform, but nothing measures up to the big ironman race.

When using visualization techniques, it is important to create a detailed and vivid mental image of your race day experience. Imagine yourself swimming smoothly through the water, cycling with strength and power, and running with determination towards the finish line. Visualize every aspect of the race, from the sights and sounds to the sensations in your body. By mentally rehearsing the race this way, you can build confidence in your abilities and develop a strong belief in your ability to succeed.

I remember swimming as I am train for Ironman one day, this was immediately after a few months from exiting the hospital, I realized I need to go find myself being at a place where I can or could visualize the Ironman race not only in the race itself but in the training so as training is my point of reference, I apply these basic rules in this lesson and I realized that just like starting a company, it had a beginning and had training. No entrepreneur was born ready, it too took training and trial and error in some cases a university degree or MBA awarded the opportunity to supplement for building the rocket as we go.

What I enjoy the most is visualizing your race day performance. However, it can also be helpful to use visualization techniques to overcome obstacles and challenges that may arise during the race. Imagine meeting difficult terrain or adverse weather conditions and visualize yourself overcoming these challenges with resilience and determination. By mentally preparing for potential obstacles in this way, you can develop a mindset of adaptability and resourcefulness that will serve you well on race day.

> As you incorporate visualization techniques into your training routine, be sure to practice regularly and consistently. Set aside time each day to visualize your race day performance and make it a priority to focus on creating a detailed and vivid mental image of success. Committing to this practice can strengthen your mental resilience and enhance your overall performance as an endurance athlete.

Visualization techniques are a valuable tool for mentally preparing for your Ironman race and enhancing your performance as an endurance athlete. By incorporating visualization into your training routine and creating detailed mental images of success, you can build confidence, overcome obstacles, and develop a powerful sense of belief in your abilities. Remember, the mind is a powerful tool, and by harnessing the power of visualization, you can achieve your goals and reach new heights of success in your Ironman journey.

Creating a Race Day Mental Script for Peak Performance

Are you ready to take your Ironman performance to the next level? Mental preparation is just as important as physical training when it comes to achieving peak performance on race day. Maximize your potential, it's essential to develop a race day mental script that will help you stay focused, motivated, and resilient throughout the grueling Ironman course.

Start by visualizing yourself crossing the finish line with a sense of accomplishment and pride. Imagine the cheers of the crowd, the feeling of satisfaction as you complete each leg of the race, and the overwhelming sense of joy as you push yourself beyond your limits. By creating a mental image of success, you are programming your mind to stay positive and determined, no matter what challenges may arise.

Next, focus on setting specific goals for each leg of the race. Whether it's improving your swim time, conquering the bike course, or maintaining a steady pace during the run, having clear objectives will keep you motivated and on track. Break down each segment of the race into manageable steps and visualize yourself achieving each goal with ease and confidence.

As you prepare for race day, practice positive self-talk and affirmations to boost your confidence and mental strength. Remind yourself of your training, your dedication, and your unwavering commitment to reaching your goals. Repeat phrases such as "I am strong," "I am determined," and "I am capable of anything I set my mind to" to reinforce a mindset of resilience and perseverance.

Finally, remember to stay present and focused during the race. Let go of any distractions or negative thoughts that may arise and stay in the moment, focusing on each breath, each stroke, and each step. Trust in your training, trust in your abilities, and trust in your mental preparation to carry you through to the finish line. With a strong race day mental script in place, you are ready to conquer the Ironman course and achieve your full potential as an endurance athlete.

Embracing Setbacks as Opportunities for Growth

In the world of sports, setbacks are inevitable. Whether it's a nagging injury, a disappointing race result, or a missed opportunity, setbacks can leave us feeling frustrated and discouraged. But what if I told you that setbacks are opportunities for growth and improvement? In this subchapter, we will explore the power of embracing setbacks as chances to learn, develop, and become stronger both mentally and physically.

When faced with a setback, it's easy to feel defeated and want to give up. But instead of viewing setbacks as obstacles, try to see them as stepping-stones on your journey to success. Every setback is an opportunity to reassess your goals, refocus your efforts, and come back stronger than ever before. Remember, it's not about how many times you fall, but how many times you get back up.

One of the key mental strategies for endurance athletes is resilience. Resilience is the ability to bounce back from setbacks, adapt to challenges, and keep moving forward. By embracing setbacks as opportunities for growth, you can cultivate resilience and develop the mental toughness needed to overcome any obstacle that comes your way. So, the next time you face a setback, remind yourself that this is just a temporary roadblock on your journey to success.

Resilience and setbacks can also teach us valuable lessons about ourselves and our training. A setback is a sign that you need to rest and recover, or it's a wake-up call to reassess your training plan. By embracing setbacks as opportunities for growth, you can learn from your mistakes, adjust, and come back even stronger in the future.

Next time you face a setback in your Ironman training, remember that it's not the end of the road but just a bend in the path. Embrace the setback as an opportunity for growth, learn from the experience, and use it to propel yourself forward. With the right mindset and mental strategies, you can turn setbacks into steppingstones on your journey to becoming an Ironman warrior.

Cultivating Mental Resilience Through Adversity

Endurance sports and mental resilience are key parts for success. The ability to push through adversity and challenges can make all the difference in achieving your goals as an athlete. Cultivating mental resilience is not an easy task, but it is essential for anyone in sports, especially for those preparing for an Ironman competition. It is during the tough moments, the moments of doubt and struggle, that mental resilience truly shines.

> Adversity is a natural part of any athletic journey. It is how we respond to adversity that defines us as athletes. Cultivating mental resilience through adversity means developing the ability to stay focused, positive, and determined even when faced with obstacles. It means finding strength in the face of challenges and using that strength to propel you forward, rather than hold you back.

One way to cultivate mental resilience is through positive self-talk. When faced with an inconvenient situation, it can be easy to fall into a negative mindset. However, by consciously choosing to speak to yourself in a positive and encouraging way, you can shift your mindset and approach challenges with a sense of determination and confidence. Remind yourself of your strengths, your past accomplishments, and your ability to overcome obstacles.

Another important aspect of cultivating mental resilience is learning to embrace failure as a learning opportunity. Setbacks and failures are a natural part of any athletic journey, but it is how we respond to them that matters most. Instead of letting failure discourage you, use it as a chance to learn and grow. Reflect on what went wrong, adjust, and come back stronger and more determined than ever.

Ironman competitions, mental resilience is just as important as physical strength. By cultivating mental resilience through adversity, you can develop the mental fortitude needed to push through the toughest moments of your race. Remember, it is not the challenges themselves that define you as an athlete, but how you respond to them. Stay focused, stay positive, and stay determined. With a strong mindset and unwavering resilience, you can conquer any challenge that comes your way.

Strategies for Managing Pain and Discomfort During the Ironman

As I set my mind to a half marathon, I view the ultramarathon, and then as an endurance athlete gearing up for the ultimate test of physical and mental strength - the Ironman - it is crucial to have a game plan in place for managing pain and discomfort throughout the grueling race. It helps you push through the toughest moments and appear victorious on the other side.

Primarily, it is important to adopt a positive mindset when faced with pain and discomfort during Ironman. Instead of viewing these challenges as roadblocks, see them as opportunities to assess your limits and grow stronger. Remind yourself of the countless hours of training you have put in and the unwavering determination that has brought you to this moment. Believe in yourself and your ability to overcome any obstacle that comes your way. So how about planning your next Ironman?

Using a powerful strategy for managing pain during Ironman is to focus on the present moment. Rather than getting caught up in thoughts of how much further you must go or how much your body is hurting, bring your attention back to the here and now. Stay present in each step, each pedal stroke, and each swim stroke. By staying in the moment, you can break the race down into manageable chunks and prevent yourself from becoming overwhelmed by the enormity of the challenge. Now these same mind games have already shown themselves in your training sessions but here you find yourself stumbling at points you had not envisioned your body would begin to fail at, but you require your mind to help you though.

Staying positive and present, it is essential to have a plan in place for dealing with pain and discomfort before race day. Practice visualization techniques that allow you to imagine yourself overcoming obstacles and pushing through pain with ease. Develop a mantra or affirmation that you can repeat to yourself when the going gets tough. And most importantly, trust in your training and preparation - you have done the work and are ready for whatever Ironman throws at you.

Like a student studying for an exam, the principle of studying is like training, the exam is racing day and so you see a question you have not seen before, and time is running out. 30 minutes on the clock before time goes up and you stumble, the principle of the matter is, apply the concepts of resilience because the blueprint is a formula used to build resilience in what and where you find yourself present.

Finally, remember that pain is temporary, but the sense of accomplishment and pride that comes from completing an Ironman lasts a lifetime.

Keep your eyes on the prize and draw strength from the knowledge that you can achieve greatness. Embrace the discomfort, push through the pain, and appear on the other side as a true Ironman warrior. You have trained your body and mind for this moment - now go out there and show the world what you are made of. You are stronger than you think, and you have what it takes to conquer Ironman. Believe in yourself, stay focused, and never give up. Ironman warrior, this is your time to shine.

Techniques for Maintaining Focus Throughout the Ironman Race

Maintaining focus throughout an Ironman race is crucial for success. As an endurance athlete, you understand the physical demands of the race, but mental preparation is equally important. By mastering techniques to stay focused, you can push through the toughest moments and achieve your goals. In this subchapter, we will explore key strategies to help you support focus throughout the Ironman race. Like a chess player strategy and begins to make predictions of how moves can be concluded, one technique for keeping focus during the Ironman race is visualization. Before the race, take time to visualize yourself crossing the finish line feeling strong and accomplished.

Visualize each segment of the race, from the swim to the bike to the run, and imagine yourself performing at your best. By visualizing success, you can boost your confidence and stay focused on your goals when the going gets tough. Back to the chess player, see your next move before it happens as the goal you have worked towards even when you have not yet paid the price.

Just like in trying to break a new world record, keeping focus during the Ironman race is setting specific, achievable goals. Break the race down into smaller segments and focus on reaching each checkpoint one at a time. By setting realistic goals for yourself, you can stay motivated and focused throughout the race. Celebrate each small victory along the way to keep your spirits high and your focus sharp.

Mindfulness is a powerful tool for supporting focus during the Ironman race. Practice staying present in the moment, focusing on your breath and the sensations in your body. By staying mindful, you can prevent distractions and keep your mind focused on the task at hand. Use mindfulness techniques to stay calm and centered, even when faced with challenges during the race.

Positive self-talk is another key technique for keeping focus throughout the Ironman race. Replace negative thoughts with positive affirmations to boost your confidence and motivation. Remind yourself of your training and preparation, and trust in your abilities to overcome any obstacles that come your way. By staying positive and encouraging yourself throughout the race, you can keep focused and push through to the finish line.

Maintaining focus throughout the Ironman race is essential for success as an endurance athlete. By using visualization, setting specific goals, practicing mindfulness, and engaging in positive self-talk, you can stay focused and motivated throughout the race. Remember to stay present in the moment, celebrate small victories, and believe in yourself and your abilities. With these techniques, you can conquer the Ironman race and achieve your goals as a warrior of endurance.

Enhancing Concentration Through Mindfulness and Meditation

The world of endurance sports, mental preparation is just as crucial as physical training. One powerful technique that can help athletes enhance their concentration and mental resilience is mindfulness and meditation. By practicing mindfulness, athletes can learn to quiet their minds, stay focused,

ITS TECHNICALLY TECHNICAL STRATEGIES

and overcome mental obstacles during grueling training sessions and competitions.

> Learning to explore how to incorporate mindfulness and meditation into your training regimen can help you become a stronger and more focused Ironman warrior. Mindfulness is the practice of being fully present and aware of your thoughts, feelings, and surroundings in the present moment.

By paying attention to your breath, sensations in your body, and the environment around you, you can cultivate a sense of calm and focus that can help you perform at your best. Incorporating mindfulness into your daily routine can help you become more attuned to your body's signals, improve your decision-making skills, and enhance your overall performance as an endurance athlete.

Meditation is another powerful tool that athletes can use to enhance their concentration and mental resilience. By setting aside just a few minutes each day to sit quietly and focus on your breath or a specific mantra, you can train your mind to stay present and centered, even during chaos or adversity. Meditation can help you develop a strong mental discipline, improve your ability to oversee stress, and boost your overall mental clarity and focus. Incorporating mindfulness and meditation into your training routine can have a profound impact on your performance as an Ironman warrior.

Have a sense of awareness and presence in the moment, you can learn to let go of distractions and negative thoughts that may hinder your progress. By training your mind to stay focused and centered, you can tap into a deep reservoir of mental strength and resilience that will carry you through the toughest challenges on race day.

As you embark on your journey to become a stronger and more focused Ironman warrior, remember that mental preparation is just as important as physical training. By incorporating mindfulness and meditation into your daily routine, you can cultivate a powerful sense of mental resilience and focus that will help you overcome any obstacle that stands in your way. Embrace the practice of mindfulness and meditation and watch as your mental strength and endurance soar to new heights.

Avoiding Mental Fatigue and Staying Sharp During Long Events

Mental fatigue can be just as challenging as physical fatigue. When taking part in long events like Ironman races, find ways to stay sharp and focused throughout the entire duration. By avoiding mental fatigue, you can improve your performance and achieve your goals with greater ease. Here are some strategies to help you stay mentally sharp during long events.

First, it is important to prioritize rest and recovery leading up to the event. Make sure to get plenty of sleep and allow your body and mind to recharge. By starting the event well-rested, you will be better equipped to manage the mental challenges that come with long-distance races.

Additionally, incorporating relaxation techniques such as meditation or deep breathing exercises can help calm your mind and keep you focused. I have seen and often seen many runners take pictures and post on social media of their running gear excited and waiting for their races to start the following day, but excitement can make you lose sleep. Sticking to what has been a part of your life for the few months or years of training is what the focus is about.

During the event, keep a positive mindset and stay present in the moment. Focus on the task at hand and avoid getting ahead of yourself by worrying about what lies ahead. By staying present, you can conserve mental energy and prevent burnout. Remember to celebrate small victories along the way, whether it's reaching a checkpoint or completing a challenging segment of the race. These small wins can help boost your confidence and motivation.

> Another key strategy for avoiding mental fatigue during long events is to break the race into smaller, more manageable segments. Instead of thinking about the entire distance you have left to cover, focus on reaching the next aid station or milestone. By setting smaller goals, you can stay motivated and keep a sense of progress throughout the event. This approach can help prevent feelings of overwhelm and keep you mentally sharp.

I understand that swimming for 4KM can be a challenge, I find that in training your muscles find their habit to survive even when your mind is processing either the victories of here after or the negative self-talks. Wherever you find yourself, incorporating mental strategies such as visualization and positive self-talk can also help you stay sharp during long events. Visualize yourself crossing the finish line and achieving your goals and remind yourself of your strengths and capabilities. By cultivating a strong mental game, you can overcome challenges and push through moments of doubt or fatigue. Remember, your mind is a powerful tool that can help you conquer even the most grueling of endurance events.

Avoiding mental fatigue and staying sharp during long events is essential for success in endurance sports. By prioritizing rest and recovery, staying present in the moment, breaking the race into smaller segments, and incorporating mental strategies, you can refine your performance and achieve your goals with confidence. Remember, the mind is a powerful force that can help you overcome any obstacle. Stay focused, stay positive, and embrace the mental challenges that come with endurance sports. You can achieve greatness – believe in yourself and push through to the finish line.

Developing a Pre-Race Ritual to Calm Nerves and Boost Confidence

Are you an endurance athlete gearing up for your next Ironman race? Do nerves get the best of you before the big event? It's time to develop a pre-race ritual that will not only calm your nerves but also boost your confidence. In this subchapter, we will explore the importance of mental preparation for Ironman athletes and how developing a ritual can set you up for success on race day.

Here are some elements to success in endurance sports like Ironman is mental toughness. It's not just about physical strength, but also about having a strong mind that can push through the challenges that come your way. By developing a pre-race ritual, you are setting yourself up for success by priming your mind for the task ahead. This ritual can help you focus, calm your nerves, and boost your confidence, all crucial elements for a successful race.

Your pre-race ritual can be anything that helps you get in the zone and feel confident and calm. It could be as simple as listening to your favorite pump-up song, doing a few minutes of deep breathing exercises, or visualizing yourself crossing the finish line. The key is to find what works for you and incorporate it into your pre-race routine. By consistently following this ritual, you will create a sense of familiarity and comfort that will help you stay focused and calm on race day.

Remember, mental preparation is just as important as physical training when it comes to endurance sports. By developing a pre-race ritual that calms your nerves and boosts your confidence, you are setting yourself up for success on race day. So, take the time to create a ritual that works for you, and watch as it transforms your mindset and performance on the course. You are an Ironman warrior, and with the right mental strategies, you can conquer any challenge that comes your way.

Staying Present and Focused During Each Leg of the Ironman

Staying present and focused during each leg of Ironman is crucial for success in this grueling endurance event. As endurance athletes, we know that our mental state plays a significant role in our performance. By staying present and focused, we can push through the pain and fatigue to reach our full potential. In this subchapter, we will explore strategies to help you stay in the moment and support your focus throughout the swim, bike, and run.

> During the swim part of the Ironman, it can be easy to get caught up in the chaos of the mass start. Stay present by focusing on your breathing and supporting a steady pace. Keep your mind clear of distractions and negative thoughts. Visualize yourself gliding effortlessly through the water, feeling strong and confident. By staying present in the moment, you can navigate the crowded waters with ease and efficiency.

As you transition to the bike leg, it's important to stay focused on your cadence and form. Avoid getting overwhelmed by the distance that still lies ahead. Break the race down into smaller, manageable segments and stay present in each moment. Remember why you started this journey in the first place and let that motivation drive you forward. Keep your mind focused on the task at hand and trust in your training and preparation.

The run part of Ironman is often where mental toughness is truly tested. As the fatigue sets in, it's essential to stay present and focused on each step. Keep your mind clear of negative thoughts and doubts. Focus on your breathing, your form, and the rhythm of your stride. Visualize yourself crossing the finish line strong and victorious. By staying present and focused during the run, you can push through the pain and exhaustion to achieve your goals.

In conclusion, staying present and focused during each leg of Ironman is key to success in this demanding endurance event. By keeping your mental composure and concentration, you can push through the challenges and obstacles that come your way. Remember to breathe, stay positive, and trust in your training. With a clear mind and focused determination, you can conquer Ironman and achieve greatness. Stay present, stay focused, and let your inner warrior shine through.

Overcoming Mental Roadblocks and Pushing Through Tough Moments

In the world of endurance sports, mental toughness is just as important as physical strength. As an Ironman athlete, you will face many challenges along the way, both on the course and in your mind. It is during these tough moments that you must learn to overcome mental roadblocks and push through with unwavering determination.

One of the key strategies for overcoming mental roadblocks is to stay present in the moment. It's easy to get overwhelmed by the magnitude of the race ahead, but by focusing on the task at hand, you can break it down into manageable parts. Take each step, each pedal stroke, each breath as it comes, and before you know it, you will be closer to the finish line.

Visualization is another powerful tool for overcoming mental roadblocks. Close your eyes and imagine yourself crossing the finish line, feeling the rush of pride and accomplishment. Picture yourself overcoming obstacles with ease and grace. By visualizing success, you can train your mind to believe in your ability to push through tough moments.

It's also important to remember that setbacks are a part of the journey. Every athlete faces challenges, whether it's a nagging injury, a tough training session, or a disappointing race. Instead of letting these setbacks derail your progress, use them as opportunities for growth and learning. Embrace the struggle and trust that it will make you stronger.

Remember that mental toughness is a skill that can be developed and honed over time. By practicing mindfulness, visualization, and resilience, you can overcome any mental roadblock that stands in your way. Stay focused, stay determined, and never lose sight of your goal. You have the strength and the courage to push through tough moments and appear victorious as an Ironman warrior.

The Importance of Mental Recovery After a Demanding Race

After completing a demanding race like Ironman, it's crucial to prioritize mental recovery just as much as physical recovery. Your mental state plays a significant role in your overall performance and well-being as an endurance athlete. Taking the time to rest and rejuvenate your mind is essential for supporting a healthy balance in your training and racing schedule.

A key reason mental recovery is so important after a race is to prevent burnout and fatigue. Pushing yourself to the limit during a race can take a toll on your mental health, and it's important to give yourself time to recover and recharge. By focusing on mental recovery, you can avoid feeling overwhelmed or exhausted from the demands of training and racing.

In addition, mental recovery can help you reflect on your performance and set new goals for the future. Taking the time to analyze your race and find areas for improvement can be a valuable learning experience. By giving yourself space to process your emotions and thoughts, you can come back stronger and more motivated for your next challenge.

Doing mental recovery planning can also help you build resilience and mental toughness as an endurance athlete. By practicing mindfulness techniques and engaging in activities that promote relaxation and stress relief, you can strengthen your mental fortitude and prepare yourself for future races. Developing a strong mental game is just as important as physical training when it comes to achieving success in endurance sports.

Ultimately, prioritizing mental recovery after a demanding race is essential for your overall well-being and long-term success as an endurance athlete. By taking care of your mental health and giving yourself the time and space to rest and recharge, you can ensure that you continue to perform at your best and achieve your goals. Remember, mental preparation is just as important as physical training in the journey to becoming an Ironman warrior.

Reflecting on Your Performance and Identifying Areas for Improvement

Reflecting on your performance and finding areas for improvement is a crucial step in the journey of any endurance athlete, especially those preparing for the grueling challenge of an Ironman race. It is through self-reflection that we can uncover our strengths and weaknesses and pave the way for growth and improvement. As you embark on your mental preparation for your Ironman, take the time to look back on your past performances with a critical eye, but also with a sense of gratitude for how far you have come.

In the sport of Ironman, every minute detail can be effective in your overall performance. By reflecting on your past races and training sessions, you can pinpoint areas where you excelled and areas where you fell short. Did you struggle with nutrition during your last race? Were you able to keep your mental focus throughout the entire event? By finding these areas for improvement, you can create a targeted plan to address them and enhance your performance on race day.

> It is important to approach this process of reflection with an open mind and a willingness to learn and grow. Instead of viewing your weaknesses as failures, see them as opportunities for growth and improvement. Remember, even the most seasoned athletes have areas where they can improve, and it is through this process of self-reflection that they are able to continue to push themselves to new heights.
>
> As you reflect on your performance and find areas for improvement, remember to celebrate your successes as well. Acknowledge the hard work and dedication that has brought you to this point and use that as motivation to continue to strive for excellence. By focusing on both your strengths and weaknesses, you can create a balanced approach to training and mental preparation that will set you up for success on race day.

In the world of Ironman racing, mental toughness is just as important as physical strength. By taking the time to reflect on your performance and find areas for improvement, you are setting yourself up for success both on and off the racecourse. Embrace this process with a cheerful outlook and a growth mindset and watch as you continue to evolve into the best version of yourself as an endurance athlete.

Setting New Mental Goals for Future Ironman Challenges

Setting new mental goals for future Ironman challenges is crucial for any endurance athlete looking to push their limits and achieve new levels of success. As athletes, it is important to constantly challenge ourselves both physically and mentally to continue growing and improving. By setting new mental goals for our Ironman races, we can push ourselves to new heights and achieve things we never thought possible.

One of the first steps in setting new mental goals for future Ironman challenges is to reflect on our past performances and find areas where we can improve. By taking the time to analyze our strengths and weaknesses, we can create a roadmap for our mental training and set specific goals to work towards. This self-reflection allows us to find any limiting beliefs or negative thought patterns that may be holding us back and replace them with positive affirmations and empowering beliefs.

Reflecting on past performances, it is important to set specific, measurable, achievable, relevant, and time-bound (SMART) goals for our mental training. By setting goals that are challenging yet attainable, we can stay motivated and focused on our training. Whether it is improving our visualization techniques, practicing mindfulness, or developing mental toughness, having clear goals in mind will keep us on track and help us stay committed to our mental training.

Another key aspect of setting new mental goals for future Ironman challenges is to stay flexible and adapt our goals as needed. As we progress in our mental training, we may meet unforeseen challenges or obstacles that require us to adjust our goals or strategies. By staying open to change and willing to adapt our goals as necessary, we can continue to grow and evolve as athletes.

Part of the new mental goals for future Ironman challenges is essential for any endurance athlete looking to improve their performance and reach new levels of success. By reflecting on past performances, setting SMART goals, and staying flexible in our approach, we can push ourselves to new heights and achieve our full potential as athletes. Remember, the mind is a powerful tool, and by harnessing its full potential, we can conquer any challenge that comes our way.

Embracing the Ironman Warrior Mindset

Embracing the Ironman Warrior mindset is essential for any athlete looking to excel in the sport of endurance racing. By adopting the mental strategies outlined in this book, you can overcome obstacles, push through pain, and achieve your goals with unwavering determination. The Ironman Warrior mindset is all about resilience, perseverance, and mental toughness – qualities that are crucial for success in the world of endurance sports.

As you navigate the challenges of training and competing in Ironman events, remember to stay focused on your goals and keep a positive mindset. Visualize your success, stay motivated, and believe in your abilities to push beyond your limits. With the Ironman Warrior mindset, you can conquer any obstacle that stands in your way and achieve greatness in your athletic pursuits.

It is important to remember that mental preparation is just as important as physical training when it comes to competing in Ironman events. By cultivating a strong mindset and adopting the strategies outlined in this book, you can overcome self-doubt, fear, and negativity, and perform at your best when it matters most.

> Embrace the Ironman Warrior mindset and watch as your performance reaches new heights. In the world of Ironman racing, mental toughness is often the factor that separates the champions from the rest. By embracing the Ironman Warrior mindset, you can develop the mental resilience and strength needed to push through the toughest of challenges and appear victorious. Remember, success in endurance sports is as much about mental fortitude as it is about physical fitness – so cultivate your warrior mindset and watch as you achieve your dreams on the racecourse.

I encourage you to embrace the Ironman Warrior mindset with open arms and a determined spirit. By adopting the mental strategies outlined in this book and committing to a mindset of unwavering determination, you can achieve greatness in the world of endurance sports. Believe in yourself, trust in your training, and never give up – for with the Ironman Warrior mindset, anything is possible. Go forth, conquer your fears, and unleash your inner warrior on the racecourse.

Acknowledging the Power of Mental Preparation in Endurance Sports

Mental preparation in endurance sports plays a crucial role in deciding an athlete's success. Whether you are training for an Ironman triathlon or any other competition, acknowledging the power of mental preparation is essential. It is not just about physical strength and endurance, but also about mental toughness and resilience. By harnessing the power of your mind, you can overcome challenges, push through the pain, and achieve your goals.

Aspects of mental preparation in endurance sports is visualization. By visualizing yourself crossing the finish line, overcoming obstacles, and pushing through the pain, you are preparing your mind for the challenges ahead. Visualization helps you build confidence, reduce anxiety, and stay focused on your goals. Take the time to visualize your race day, from the moment you wake up to the moment you cross the finish line. See yourself overcoming obstacles with ease and celebrating your success at the end.

Another important aspect of mental preparation is setting goals and creating a plan to achieve them. Whether your goal is to finish your first Ironman or to improve your personal best, having a clear goal in mind will give you direction and motivation. Break down your goal into smaller, achievable steps and create a training plan that will help you reach your target. By setting specific, measurable, achievable, relevant, and time-bound (SMART) goals, you will stay focused and motivated throughout your training.

In addition to visualization and goal setting, mental preparation in endurance sports also involves developing a positive mindset. It is important to cultivate a cheerful outlook, believe in yourself, and stay optimistic, even in the face of challenges. Remember that your mind is a powerful tool that can either propel you forward or hold you back. By staying positive and focusing on your strengths, you will be better equipped to oversee the difficulties of endurance sports.

The power of mental preparation in endurance sports cannot be underestimated. By acknowledging the importance of visualization, goal setting, and developing a positive mindset, you can enhance your performance, overcome obstacles, and achieve your goals. Remember that mental toughness is just as important as physical strength in endurance sports. With the right mental strategies and a cheerful outlook, you can become an Ironman warrior and conquer any challenge that comes your way.

Encouraging Continued Growth and Development as an Ironman Warrior

As an Ironman warrior, the journey towards greatness is never truly complete. It is a continuous process of growth and development, both physically and mentally. To truly excel in the world of endurance sports, it is essential to focus on encouraging and nurturing your ongoing growth as an athlete. By adopting a mindset of constant improvement, you can push past your limits and achieve new levels of success in your Ironman journey.

> Empower yourself as an Ironman warrior by setting ambitious yet achievable goals. This not only allows you to track your progress but also gives you a sense of control and motivation to push yourself further. Whether it is improving your swim time, increasing your biking distance, or enhancing your mental resilience, having clear goals keeps you focused and committed to your training.

It is essential to cultivate a positive and resilient mindset as an Ironman warrior. Endurance sports like Ironman require mental toughness and strong determination to overcome challenges and obstacles. By practicing positive self-talk, visualization techniques, and mindfulness exercises, you can strengthen your mental fortitude and prepare yourself for the rigors of competition.

Another key aspect of encouraging continued growth and development as an Ironman warrior is seeking opportunities for learning and improvement. Whether attending workshops or seminars or seeking guidance from experienced coaches and athletes, there is always room to expand your knowledge and skill set. By staying open to innovative ideas and perspectives, you can continue to evolve and grow as an athlete.

Becoming a victorious Ironman warrior is a marathon, not a sprint. It requires dedication, perseverance, and a willingness to push yourself beyond your comfort zone. By embracing a continual growth and development mindset, you can unlock your full potential as an athlete and achieve greatness in the world of endurance sports. Remember, the only limits that exist are the ones you place on yourself – so dare to dream big and never stop striving for excellence as an Ironman warrior.

Inspiring Others to Harness the Power of Their Minds for Athletic Success

Are you ready to unlock the full potential of your mind and achieve athletic success like never before? In this subchapter, we will explore the incredible power of the mind in the world of sports, specifically focusing on mental preparation for your Ironman journey. By harnessing the power of your mind, you can overcome obstacles, push through barriers, and achieve feats you never thought possible. It is time to inspire others to tap into the limitless potential of their minds and reach new heights in their athletic endeavors.

One key factor in athletic success is mental preparation. By training your mind just as diligently as you train your body, you can cultivate a winning mindset that will propel you toward your goals. Visualizing success, staying focused, and supporting a positive attitude are all essential components of mental preparation for your Ironman journey. When you believe in yourself and your abilities, you can conquer any challenge that comes your way.

It is important to remember that success in sports is not just about physical strength and endurance but also mental toughness. By developing mental resilience and grit, you can push through pain, fatigue, and self-doubt to achieve greatness. Please share your experiences of overcoming obstacles and achieving success through sheer determination and mental strength to inspire others to harness the power of their minds.

In the world of Ironman racing, mental toughness is often the deciding factor between victory and defeat. By inspiring others to harness the power of their minds, you can help them cultivate the mental resilience they need to succeed in this demanding sport. Encourage your fellow athletes to embrace the challenges, push past their limits, and tap into their inner strength to achieve their goals. Together, we can create a community of Ironman warriors who inspire and support each other on their journey to greatness.

Let us come together and inspire others to harness the power of their minds for athletic success. By sharing our experiences, offering support and encouragement, and leading by example, we can help each other reach new heights in our Ironman journeys. With a strong mind and unwavering determination, there is no limit to what we can achieve. Let us embrace the power of our minds and become the Ironman warriors we were always meant to be, knowing that we are part of a supportive community that inspires and uplifts each other.

LESSON 4

Leading Resiliently

Cultivating Resilience in Leadership

> The first step in navigating crises with confidence is to acknowledge and accept the situation. Denying or avoiding the reality of a crisis will only prolong the pain and make it more difficult to find a solution. By facing the crisis head-on and accepting the challenges it presents, business owners can begin to formulate a plan of action and move forward with clarity and purpose.

> *"Try a little harder every day until you win."*
>
> – ETHAN R. ESBACH

Leading by Example during Difficult Times

In times of crisis and uncertainty, it is crucial for business owners to lead by example. As the captain of the ship, your team looks to you for guidance and reassurance during difficult times. By demonstrating resilience and a positive mindset, you can inspire and motivate your employees to overcome challenges and navigate through turbulent waters. Leading by example means staying calm and composed in the face of adversity. It means showing strength and determination even when the odds are stacked against you. By maintaining a resilient mindset, you can in still confidence in your team and show them that together, you can overcome any obstacle that comes your way.

During difficult times, it is important for business owners to communicate openly and honestly with their employees. By sharing your thoughts and concerns, you can create a sense of unity and trust within your team. Be transparent about the challenges you are facing and encourage your employees to do the same. This will foster a culture of collaboration and support, enabling everyone to work together towards a common goal. Leading by example also means taking care of yourself and prioritizing your own well-being. As a business owner, it can be easy to neglect self-care in favour of focusing on the needs of your company. However, it is important to remember that you cannot pour from an empty cup. By practicing self-care and setting boundaries, you can recharge and replenish your energy, enabling you to lead your team effectively during difficult times.

Leading by example during difficult times is major for business owners who want to cultivate resilience in their personal growth and development. By demonstrating a positive mindset, open communication, and self-care, you can inspire and motivate your team to overcome challenges and emerge stronger than ever. Remember, as the leader of your company, your actions speak louder than words. Show your team that you have the strength and determination to weather any storm, and they will follow your lead toward success.

Fostering a Resilient Company Culture

In today's fast-paced and ever-changing business landscape, fostering a resilient company culture is essential for the success and longevity of any organization. As business owners, it is crucial to create an environment where employees feel supported, empowered, and able to bounce back from setbacks with a positive mindset. By cultivating a resilient company culture, businesses can not only weather the storms of uncertainty and challenges but also thrive in the face of adversity.

> One of the key aspects of fostering a resilient company culture is promoting open communication and transparency within the organization. Encouraging employees to share their thoughts, concerns, and ideas creates a sense of trust and collaboration that is essential for building resilience. When employees feel heard and valued, they are more likely to feel motivated and engaged, even in the face of difficult situations. By creating a culture of open communication, business owners can lay the foundation for a resilient and adaptive workplace.

Another important aspect of fostering a resilient company culture is providing opportunities for professional development and growth. Investing in the personal and professional growth of employees not only enhances their skills and abilities but also increases their resilience in the face of challenges. By offering training, mentorship programs, and opportunities for advancement, business owners can empower their employees to overcome obstacles and thrive in their roles.

A culture that encourages continuous learning and development is key to building resilience in the workplace. In addition to promoting open communication and professional development, fostering a resilient company culture also involves recognizing and celebrating achievements, both big and small. By acknowledging and rewarding the hard work and accomplishments of employees, business owners can boost morale, motivation, and resilience within the organization. Celebrating successes, no matter how small, helps to create a positive and supportive work environment that encourages employees to persevere and overcome obstacles.

Ultimately, fostering a resilient company culture requires a commitment to creating a supportive, inclusive, and growth-oriented environment where employees feel empowered to face challenges head-on. By promoting open communication, providing opportunities for professional development, and celebrating achievements, business owners can cultivate a culture of resilience that enables their organization to thrive in the face of adversity. In today's competitive business landscape, building a resilient company culture is not just an option – it is a necessity for long-term success and sustainability.

Navigating Crises with Confidence

In the fast-paced world of business, unexpected crises can strike at any moment, leaving business owners feeling overwhelmed and underprepared. However, with the right mindset and strategies in place, it is possible to navigate these challenges with confidence and resilience. In this subchapter, we will explore how business owners can develop a resilient mindset to overcome crises and emerge stronger than ever.

> The first step in navigating crises with confidence is to acknowledge and accept the situation. Denying or avoiding the reality of a crisis will only prolong the pain and make it more difficult to find a solution. By facing the crisis head-on and accepting the challenges it presents, business owners can begin to formulate a plan of action and move forward with clarity and purpose.

Another key aspect of navigating crises with confidence is to leverage the power of perspective. Instead of viewing a crisis as insurmountable, business owners can choose to see it as an opportunity for growth and learning. By shifting their perspective and reframing the situation in a positive light, business owners can approach the crisis with a sense of optimism and determination.

Therefore, building a strong support network is essential for navigating crises with confidence. Surrounding oneself with trusted advisors, mentors, and colleagues can provide valuable insights and perspectives during challenging times. By seeking guidance and support from others, business owners can gain new perspectives and develop creative solutions to overcome the crisis at hand.

In time navigating crises with confidence requires a combination of resilience, adaptability, and determination. By developing a resilient mindset and implementing strategies to overcome challenges, business owners can not only survive crises but thrive in the face of adversity. With the right tools and support in place, business owners can confidently navigate any crisis that comes their way and emerge stronger and more resilient than ever before.

Silencing the Inner Critic -Cultivating Positive Affirmations

If you're tired of listening to that pesky inner critic constantly putting you down, then you've come to the right place. It's time to kick that negative self-talk to the curb and start embracing a more positive mindset. First things first, let's talk about what positive affirmations are. These are short, positive statements that you repeat to yourself regularly to challenge and overcome self-limiting beliefs. Think of them as little pep tells you give yourself to boost your confidence and motivation.

Now, I know what you're thinking - isn't this just a bunch of fluffy nonsense? Well, not exactly. Positive affirmations have been proven to rewire our brains, helping us shift our mindset from negative to positive. So, it's time to channel your inner cheerleader and start practicing some self-love.

When creating your positive affirmations, it's important to keep them specific, realistic, and believable. Instead of saying, "I am the best at everything," try something like, "I am capable of handling whatever challenges come my way." Remember, the goal is to build yourself up, not set yourself up for failure. So, grab a sticky note, write down a few affirmations, and start repeating them to yourself daily. It may feel a little silly at first, but trust me, the results will be worth it. Before you know it, that inner critic will be silenced, and you'll be well on your way to a more positive and confident mindset.

Practicing Mindfulness to Quiet the Inner Critic

Are you tired of constantly hearing that nagging voice in your head telling you that you're not good enough? Well, it's time to show that inner critic whose boss by practicing mindfulness. That's right, by staying present in the moment and focusing on the here and now, you can quiet that negative self-talk and finally find some peace of mind.

Imagine your inner critic as a pesky little gremlin sitting on your shoulder, constantly whispering negative thoughts in your ear. Well, it's time to flick that gremlin off your shoulder and replace those negative thoughts with positive affirmations. By practicing mindfulness, you can train your mind to focus on the present moment and let go of those self-limiting beliefs that are holding you back.

One way to practice mindfulness is by taking a few deep breaths and focusing on the sensations of your breath entering and leaving your body. This simple exercise can help quiet your mind and bring you back to the present moment, where your inner critic has no power over you. So, take a deep breath, let go of those negative thoughts, and remember that you are worthy of love and acceptance just as you are.

Another way to silence your inner critic is by practicing self-compassion. Treat yourself with the same kindness and understanding that you would show to a friend who is struggling. Remember, you are your own worst critic, so it's time to start being your own best friend instead. By practicing self-compassion, you can quiet that inner critic and start to build a more positive relationship with yourself.

So, the next time your inner critic starts to rear its ugly head, remember to practice mindfulness and self-compassion. By staying present in the moment and treating yourself with kindness, you can finally silence that negative self-talk and start living a more positive and fulfilling life. It's time to take control of your thoughts and show that inner critic who's boss once and for all!

Embracing Imperfection and Self-Acceptance

Do you ever feel like you're constantly battling with your inner critic, that little voice in your head that loves to point out every flaw and mistake you make? Trust me, you're not alone. In fact, most adults struggle with negative self-talk daily. But what if I told you that embracing imperfection and practicing self-acceptance could be the key to silencing that pesky critic once and for all?

Let's face it, nobody's perfect. We all have our quirks, flaws, and imperfections. And you know what? That's what makes us unique and special. So instead of constantly striving for perfection, why not embrace your imperfections and celebrate them? After all, life would be boring if we were all cookie-cutter copies of each other.

Self-acceptance is all about loving yourself unconditionally, flaws and all. It means embracing the parts of yourself that you may not love and learning to be okay with them. So, the next time your inner critic starts chirping away, remind yourself that it's okay to be imperfect.

In fact, imperfection is what makes you human! One of the best ways to practice self-acceptance is to surround yourself with people who love and accept you for who you are. Surround yourself with friends and family who lift you up and remind you of your worth. And remember, a little self-love goes a long way.

So go ahead, embrace your imperfections, practice self-acceptance, and show that inner critic who's boss. Life's too short to be constantly at war with yourself. Remember, you are enough just as you are. So let go of those self-limiting beliefs and negative self-talk, and start embracing the wonderful, imperfect person that you are. We all want to live largely, but living large happens with planning for when things become a little slow-paced in life and the body begins to decide that bedtime is no longer at 11 pm but at 8 pm. Those years need to be planned for as retirement is not for when it happens it's for ensuring that when it happens, it happens with feeling comfortable.

Importance of Retirement Planning

Retirement planning is a crucial aspect of financial fitness for business owners. Many entrepreneurs focus on growing their businesses and often overlook the importance of planning for their retirement. However, retirement planning is essential for ensuring a secure financial future and keeping a comfortable lifestyle in retirement. By starting to plan for retirement early on, business owners can take advantage of compounding interest and maximize their savings for retirement.

One of the key reasons why retirement planning is important for business owners is to avoid financial struggles in retirement. Without proper planning, business owners may find themselves unable to support their current standard of living once they retire. By setting aside funds for retirement and creating a financial plan, business owners can ensure that they have enough money to cover their living expenses and enjoy their retirement years without financial stress.

Another important reason for business owners to focus on retirement planning is to take advantage of tax benefits and incentives. There are various retirement savings options available to business owners, such as 401(k) plans, SEP IRAs, and SIMPLE IRAs, which offer tax advantages and incentives for saving for retirement. By using these retirement savings options, business owners can reduce their tax liability and grow their retirement savings more effectively.

Financial security and tax benefits and retirement planning can also provide business owners with peace of mind and a sense of control over their financial future. By creating a retirement plan and setting specific goals for retirement savings, business owners can feel confident that they are taking the necessary steps to secure their financial future. This sense of control and peace of mind can help business owners reduce stress and anxiety about their retirement years.

Overall, retirement planning is a critical part of financial fitness for business owners. By taking the time to create a retirement plan, set goals, and use retirement savings options, business owners can ensure a secure financial future and enjoy a comfortable retirement. With the guidance of a financial coach, business owners can develop a personalized retirement plan that aligns with their financial goals and helps them achieve financial security in retirement.

Retirement Plan Options for Business Owners

When it comes to planning for retirement as a business owner, there are several options available to help you secure your financial future. Retirement plan options specifically designed for business owners are many with different options. By understanding these options, you can make informed decisions that align with your financial goals and provide for a comfortable retirement.

One popular retirement plan possibility for business owners is the Simplified Employee Pension (SEP) IRA. I will be using Canada or United States and how their structures accommodate but for South African, the SASSA grants form a base or pensions. The SEP plan allows business owners to contribute up to 25% of their net earnings, up to a certain limit, to a retirement account for themselves and their employees. SEPs are easy to set up and administer, making them a convenient choice for small businesses looking to provide retirement benefits to their employees.

Another retirement plan choice for business owners is the Solo 401(k). This plan is designed for self-employed individuals or business owners with no employees other than a spouse. With a Solo 401(k), you can contribute up to $58,000 per year (for 2021) or $64,500 if you are age 50 or older. This plan offers higher contribution limits than a SEP IRA and allows for both employee and employer contributions.

For business owners looking to maximize their retirement savings, a Defined Benefit Plan may be a suitable option. This plan allows business owners to contribute larger amounts to their retirement account than other plans, potentially providing a higher level of retirement income. Defined Benefit Plans are ideal for business owners with steady income and the ability to make consistent contributions over time.

In addition to these options, business owners may also consider setting up a SIMPLE IRA or a Profit-Sharing Plan. These plans offer flexibility in contribution amounts and may be suitable for businesses of varied sizes and structures. By exploring the various retirement plan options available, business owners can choose the plan that best fits their financial situation and retirement goals. It is important to consult with a financial advisor or retirement planning expert to figure out the most appropriate plan for your specific needs. Formulating these plans into meaningful approaches for your retirement will help you stay organized and support a lifestyle when the time comes.

Maximizing Retirement Savings

Retirement planning is a crucial aspect of financial fitness for business owners. To maximize retirement savings, it is important to start planning early and consistently contribute to retirement accounts. By taking steps towards saving for retirement, business owners can ensure a comfortable and secure future for themselves and their families.

> One effective way to maximize retirement savings is to take advantage of employer-sponsored retirement plans, such as 401(k) or 403(b) plans. These plans allow business owners to contribute a part of their income on a pre-tax basis, which can help reduce their taxable income while saving for retirement. Employers offer matching contributions, which can significantly boost retirement savings over time.

Another strategy for maximizing retirement savings is to diversify investments within retirement accounts. By spreading investments across different asset classes, such as stocks, bonds, and real estate, business owners can reduce risk and potentially increase returns. It is important to regularly review and adjust investment allocations based on market conditions and retirement goals.

Some employer-sponsored retirement plans, where business owners may also consider opening individual retirement accounts (IRAs) or Roth IRAs. These accounts offer tax advantages and flexibility in terms of investment options. By contributing to both employer-sponsored plans and individual retirement accounts, business owners can further increase their retirement savings potential.

Overall, maximizing retirement savings requires a combination of consistent contributions, diversified investments, and strategic planning. By taking an initiative-taking approach to retirement planning, business owners can secure their financial future and enjoy a comfortable retirement. Financial coaching can play a key role in helping business owners navigate the complexities of retirement planning and develop a personalized strategy for maximizing their retirement savings.

Planning for the Future of Your Business

Planning for the future of your business is crucial for long-term success and sustainability. As a business owner, it is important to have an unobstructed vision of where you want your business to go and how you plan to get there. This involves setting goals, creating a strategic plan, and implementing strategies to achieve those goals. By planning for the future, you can predict potential challenges and opportunities, and be better prepared to navigate them effectively.

One key aspect of planning for the future of your business is setting financial goals. This involves deciding how much revenue you want to generate, how much profit you want to make, and how much you want to invest back into your business. By setting specific, measurable, achievable, relevant, and time-bound (SMART) financial goals, you can track your progress and adjust as needed to stay on track.

> Another important aspect of planning for the future of your business is creating a budget. A budget is a financial plan that outlines your expected income and expenses over a specific period. By creating a budget, you can ensure that you are spending within your means, name areas where you can cut costs or increase revenue and make informed decisions about how to distribute your financial resources. In addition

to setting financial goals and creating a budget, it is important to regularly review and update your business plan.

Your business plan should be a living document that evolves as your business grows and changes. By regularly reviewing and updating your business plan, you can ensure that you are staying on track to achieve your goals, find areas where you may need to adjust, and make informed decisions about the future direction of your business.

Future planning of your business is essential for long-term success and sustainability. By setting financial goals, creating a budget, and regularly reviewing and updating your business plan, you can ensure that you are prepared to navigate the challenges and opportunities that come your way, and continue to grow and thrive in the future.

Succession Planning Strategies

Succession planning is a crucial aspect of any business, especially for business owners looking to secure the future of their company. Various strategies that can help business owners effectively plan for the transition of leadership within their organization. By implementing these strategies, business owners can ensure a smooth and successful transfer of power, preserving the legacy of their business for years to come.

One key strategy in succession planning is finding and developing potential successors within the organization. This involves assessing current employees for their leadership qualities, skills, and potential to take on higher roles within the company. By providing training and mentorship opportunities to these individuals, business owners can groom them for future leadership positions, ensuring a seamless transition when the time comes for a change in leadership.

Other important strategy is creating a detailed succession plan that outlines the steps and timeline for the transfer of power. This plan should include key milestones, responsibilities, and contingencies in case of unforeseen circumstances. By having a clear roadmap in place, business owners can effectively communicate their vision for succession with all stakeholders and ensure a smooth transition process.

It is also essential for business owners to consider external candidates as potential successors. This can bring fresh perspectives and innovative ideas to the organization, ensuring its continued growth and success. By networking and building relationships with potential external candidates, business owners can expand their pool of talent and find the best fit for the future leadership of their company.

One more is regular reviews and updates of the succession plan are critical to its success. Business owners should regularly assess the progress of potential successors, review their development plans, and make any necessary adjustments to ensure that the plan stays relevant and effective. By staying initiative-taking and adaptable, business owners can ensure that their succession plan is well-prepared to manage any changes or challenges that may arise in the future.

Exiting Your Business on Your Terms

Exiting your business on your own terms is a crucial step for any business owner. Whether you are planning to retire, pursue other interests, or simply want to move on to the next chapter of your life, it is important to have a clear plan in place with guidance on how to successfully exit your business while maximizing your financial returns and ensuring a smooth transition for both you and your employees.

One of the first steps in exiting your business on your terms is to set up a clear timeline for your departure. This timeline should consider your personal goals, financial needs, and the overall health of your business. By setting a timeline, you can create a roadmap for the steps you need to take to exit your business in a strategic and organized manner.

Another important aspect of exiting your business on your terms is to assess the value of your business. This involves conducting a thorough evaluation of your assets, liabilities, and future cash flows to find the true worth of your business. By understanding the value of your business, you can make informed decisions about the best way to exit, whether through a sale, merger, or succession plan.

Once you have a clear timeline and understanding of your business's value, it is important to develop a comprehensive exit strategy. This strategy should outline the steps you need to take to exit your business successfully, including finding potential buyers or successors, negotiating terms of sale, and developing a plan for transitioning leadership. By having a well-defined exit strategy, you can ensure a smooth and successful transition for all parties involved.

Exiting your business on your terms is a great aspect of being a successful business owner. By showing a clear timeline, assessing the value of your business, and developing a comprehensive exit strategy, you can ensure a smooth and successful transition that maximizes your financial returns and sets you up for success in your next chapter. Remember, it is never too early to start planning for your exit, so start taking steps today to secure your financial future.

Regular Financial Check-Ins

Regular financial check-ins are an essential practice for business owners looking to keep financial stability and make informed decisions. These check-ins involve reviewing financial statements, assessing cash flow, and setting financial goals to track progress over time. By consistently checking and evaluating your business's financial health, you can identify potential issues early on and make necessary adjustments to stay on track towards your financial goals.

One key aspect of regular financial check-ins is reviewing financial statements, including income statements, balance sheets, and cash flow statements. These statements provide a snapshot of your business's financial performance and can help you find trends, patterns, and areas of improvement. By understanding these financial statements, you can make more informed decisions about budgeting, investing, and strategic planning for your business.

Assessing cash flow is another part of regular financial check-ins. Cash flow is the lifeblood of any business and monitoring it regularly can help you ensure that your business has enough cash on hand to meet its financial obligations, such as paying bills, employees, and suppliers. By analyzing your cash flow, you can identify potential cash flow gaps and take proactive steps to address them before they become a problem. Setting financial goals is also an important part of regular financial check-ins. By establishing clear, measurable financial goals for your business, you can track your progress over time and adjust as needed to stay on track towards achieving those goals. Whether your goals are related to increasing revenue, reducing expenses, or improving profitability, regular financial check-ins can help you stay focused and motivated to achieve them.

Regular financial check-ins are a vital practice for business owners looking to maintain financial health and make informed decisions. By reviewing financial statements, assessing cash flow, and setting financial goals, you can identify potential issues early on, make necessary adjustments, and stay on track toward achieving your financial goals. By prioritizing regular financial check-ins, you can ensure that your business remains financially fit and well-positioned for long-term success.

Adjusting Your Financial Plan as Needed

Adjusting your financial plan as needed means maintaining financial health for business owners. As your business evolves and market conditions change, it is essential to regularly review and update your financial plan to ensure it remains aligned with your goals and objectives. By staying proactive and flexible in your approach to financial planning, you can better navigate unexpected challenges and capitalize on new opportunities.

One more aspect is adjusting your financial plan is conducting regular financial check-ins. This involves reviewing your financial statements, cash flow projections, and budget to assess your current financial situation. By tracking your financial performance against your goals, you can identify any areas that may need adjustment and make informed decisions about how to best allocate your resources.

After regular check-ins, it is important to consider external factors that may impact your financial plan. This includes changes in the market, regulatory environment, and competitive landscape. By staying informed about these external factors and how they may affect your business, you can proactively adjust your financial plan to mitigate risks and capitalize on opportunities.

Another important aspect of adjusting your financial plan is seeking the guidance of a financial coach. A financial coach can provide valuable insights and expertise to help you make informed decisions about your finances. By collaborating with a coach, you can develop a comprehensive financial plan that is tailored to your specific needs and goals and receive ongoing support and guidance as you navigate the complexities of business ownership.

Adjusting your financial plan implies financial fitness for business owners. By staying initiative-taking, flexible, and informed, you can ensure that your financial plan remains aligned with your goals and objectives and adapt to changing market conditions. By conducting regular financial check-ins, considering external factors, and seeking the guidance of a financial coach, you can navigate the challenges of business ownership with confidence and achieve long-term financial success.

Celebrating Financial Milestones

In the journey of building a successful business, it is important to celebrate financial milestones along the way. These milestones serve as a reminder of the hard work and dedication that has gone into growing the business and achieving financial success. Whether it is reaching a specific revenue goal, securing a new investment, or paying off debt, each milestone is a cause for celebration and reflection on the progress made.

A benefit of celebrating financial milestones is the motivation and inspiration it provides to both business owners and their teams. Recognizing and celebrating achievements boosts morale and encourages continued effort towards reaching future goals. It also reinforces a positive mindset and helps to build a culture of success within the organization.

> Celebrating financial milestones also offers an opportunity for reflection and evaluation of the business's financial health. By acknowledging and celebrating achievements, business owners can gain valuable insights into what strategies and tactics have been successful in driving financial growth. This reflection can inform future decision-making and help to set new financial goals that align with the overall vision and goals of the business. Furthermore, celebrating financial milestones can help to strengthen relationships with stakeholders, including investors, partners, and employees. Sharing successes and achievements with these key individuals can foster a sense of pride and loyalty towards the business. It also shows transparency and accountability in financial management, which can help to build trust and credibility within the business community.

Overall, celebrating financial milestones is an important practice for business owners seeking to maintain financial fitness and drive continued success. By recognizing and acknowledging achievements, business owners can boost morale, gain valuable insights, and strengthen relationships with stakeholders. It is an opportunity to reflect on past accomplishments and set new goals that will propel the business towards even greater financial success in the future.

I understand that certain aspects of toughness are needed to meet physical fitness goals. Part of life requires financial fitness, which is another form of resilience we must understand because we must admit that struggling financially can become discouraging.

The Importance of Financial Fitness

Financial fitness is not just a choice; it is a necessity for the success of any business owner. It is the foundation upon which all other aspects of a business are built. Without a solid understanding of financial principles and practices, business owners may struggle to make informed decisions that could impact the future of their company. In this subchapter, we will explore the importance of financial fitness for business owners and how it can profoundly affect their businesses' success.

One of the primary reasons why financial fitness is so crucial for business owners is that it enables them to make informed decisions about their finances. By understanding critical economic concepts such as cash flow management, budgeting (e.g., setting a marketing budget for a new product launch), and financial forecasting (e.g., predicting sales for the next quarter), business owners can better plan and ensure the long-term viability of their businesses. Without this knowledge, business owners may find themselves making hasty decisions that could have detrimental effects on their bottom line.

Financial fitness can also help business owners name potential business risks and opportunities. By regularly reviewing their financial statements and performance metrics, business owners can spot trends and patterns that may show areas of concern or areas for growth. This initiative-taking approach to economic management can help business owners mitigate risks and capitalize on opportunities before they become significant issues.

In helping business owners make informed decisions and identify risks and opportunities, financial fitness also plays a role in securing funding for their businesses. Lenders and investors are more likely to trust business owners who understand their finances and can provide accurate and timely financial information. By maintaining financial fitness, business owners can increase their chances of securing the funding they need to grow and expand their businesses.

Financial fitness is a cornerstone of business success. By investing time and effort into understanding critical financial principles and practices, business owners can set themselves up for long-term success and sustainability. Through proper economic management, business owners can make informed decisions, identify risks and opportunities, and secure the funding they need to achieve their business goals.

Common Financial Challenges for Business Owners

As a business owner, you will likely face various financial challenges affecting your business's success. Understanding these familiar challenges and how to address them is valuable to ensuring your business's economic health. These are some of the most common financial challenges business owners face, and strategies for overcoming them are provided. Cash flow management is one of the most common financial challenges for business owners. Cash flow refers to the movement of money in and out of your business, and poor cash flow management can lead to various problems, including the inability to pay bills on time, missed growth opportunities, and even business failure. Many businesses have fallen into the trap of cash flow issues.

To address this challenge, business owners should show a cash flow budget, monitor cash flow regularly, and take steps to improve cash flow, such as reducing expenses or increasing sales. Not spending more than you make is not always an option since the cost of ensuring a business remains compliant has hidden costs, leading to another common financial challenge for business owners: managing debt. Many businesses rely on debt to finance their operations, but excessive debt can be a burden that hinders growth and profitability. Business owners should work to manage debt effectively by developing a debt repayment plan, negotiating with creditors to reduce interest rates or payment terms, and avoiding taking on new debt unless necessary.

> Tax planning is another financial challenge that business owners often face. Taxes can be a significant expense for businesses, and not planning for them properly can result in penalties, fines, or even legal trouble. Business owners should work with a tax professional to develop a tax strategy that minimizes tax liability while complying with the tax laws of that country. Investing in the right areas is necessary for business success, but many business owners struggle to make wise investment decisions. Whether it is investing in new technology, marketing, or expanding operations, business owners should carefully evaluate potential investments to ensure they align with their business goals and will provide a positive return on investment.

Finally, but not the least of the possible concerns is succession planning, a common financial challenge for business owners, particularly those nearing retirement age. Planning for the future of your business, whether through transferring ownership to a family member, selling the business, or winding down operations, is relevant for ensuring a smooth transition and protecting the business's financial stability. Business owners should operate with a financial coach or advisor to develop a succession plan that meets their goals and protects the long-term economic health of the business. As a business coach, I aim to help my clients cultivate resilience, enabling them to overcome challenges and acquire valuable knowledge. Education and coaching offer numerous benefits that aid individuals in grasping and applying business principles for desirable outcomes serving the needs of their future generations.

Benefits of Financial Coaching for Business Owners

Financial coaching for business owners can provide many benefits that can help improve a business's overall economic health and success. One key benefit is the ability to understand better the financial aspects of running a business. Many business owners may not have a background in finance, so working with a financial coach can help them navigate complex economic concepts and make more informed decisions.

Another benefit of financial coaching for business owners is setting and achieving financial goals. A financial coach can help business owners identify their financial goals, create a plan to achieve them and hold them accountable. This can help business owners stay focused and motivated to reach their financial objectives.

Financial coaching can also help business owners improve their fiscal management skills. By collaborating with a financial coach, business owners can learn how to track and manage their finances better, create and stick to a budget, and make strategic financial decisions that align with their business goals. This can lead to increased profitability and long-term financial stability for the business.

Financial coaching can give business owners a fresh perspective on their financial situation. Sometimes, business owners may be too close to their finances to see the bigger picture or identify areas for improvement. A financial coach can offer an outside perspective and help business owners see their finances in a new light, leading to more effective financial strategies and solutions.

Overall, financial coaching for business owners can be a valuable investment in the success and sustainability of a business. By gaining a better understanding of their finances, setting, and achieving financial goals, improving economic management skills, and gaining a fresh perspective, business owners can position themselves for long-term success and growth.

Identifying Short-Term and Long-Term Financial Goals

Identifying short-term and long-term financial goals will help you achieve economic success as a business owner. Short-term goals can be completed within a year or less, while long-term goals may take several years. By clearly defining your financial goals, you can create a roadmap for your business and work towards achieving them effectively.

Short-term financial goals for a business may include increasing cash flow, reducing operating expenses, or paying off high-interest debt. These goals are typically focused on improving the company's economic health in the immediate future. By setting specific, measurable, achievable, relevant, and time-bound (SMART) goals, business owners can track their progress and adjust as needed to stay on track.

Long-term financial goals for a business may include saving for retirement, expanding into new markets, or acquiring another company. These goals require careful planning and may involve more significant financial investments. By setting long-term goals, business owners can create a vision for their business's future and work towards building a solid financial foundation for years to come.

Business owners should consider short-term and long-term objectives when identifying financial goals. Short-term goals can help provide immediate benefits and improve the business's economic health, while long-term goals can eventually help create a sustainable and successful business. By balancing short-term and long-term goals, business owners can create a comprehensive financial plan that addresses current needs and future aspirations.

Basically, identifying short-term and long-term financial goals is critical to achieving financial fitness as a business owner. By setting specific, measurable goals and creating a clear roadmap for success, business owners can work towards building a solid economic foundation for their business. Whether focusing on short-term improvements or long-term growth, having an unclouded vision for the future can help business owners stay on track and achieve their financial goals.

Creating a Realistic Budget

Creating a realistic budget is pivotal for any business's financial health and success. A budget is a roadmap for managing expenses, tracking revenue, and making informed financial decisions. This subchapter will discuss the critical steps to creating a realistic budget that aligns with your business goals and objectives.

The first step in creating a realistic budget is to gather all relevant financial information. This includes past financial statements, sales forecasts, and other applicable financial data. By having a clear understanding of your financial situation, you can create a budget that is based on accurate and up-to-date information.

Once you have gathered all relevant financial information, the next step is identifying your business's fixed and variable expenses. Fixed expenses, such as rent and utilities, remain constant month-to-month. Variable costs, on the other hand, fluctuate based on business activity, such as inventory purchases or marketing expenses. By categorizing your expenses into fixed and variable categories, you can better plan for and allocate funds in your budget.

After identifying your expenses, the next step is to forecast your revenue. This involves estimating how much your business will generate over a certain period, typically a month or a year. A realistic revenue forecast ensures your budget is based on achievable financial goals and objectives.

Finally, once you have gathered all relevant financial information, categorized your expenses, and forecasted your revenue, it is time to create your budget. Your budget should outline your expected income, costs, and profit margins for a specific period. Regularly monitoring and adjusting your budget ensures that your business stays on track financially and achieves its goals. Creating a realistic budget is a critical component of financial fitness for business owners, and by following these steps, you can set your business up for long-term economic success.

Strategies for Achieving Financial Goals

Strategies for achieving financial goals are essential for business owners looking to improve their financial fitness. One key strategy is setting specific, measurable, achievable, relevant, and time-bound (SMART) goals. By creating SMART goals, business owners can clearly define their goals and track their progress. This helps them stay focused and motivated to reach their financial objectives.

A critical strategy for achieving financial goals is creating a budget and sticking to it. A budget helps business owners understand their cash flow, identify areas where they can cut costs, and allocate funds toward their financial goals. By consistently monitoring their budget and adjusting as needed, business owners can stay on track to achieve their financial goals.

Diversifying income streams is another effective strategy for achieving financial goals. Relying on only one source of income can leave business owners vulnerable to economic downturns or industry changes. By diversifying their income streams through new products, services, or partnerships, business owners can increase their financial stability and work towards achieving their long-term financial goals.

Investing wisely is also crucial for achieving financial goals. Business owners should educate themselves on different investment options, such as stocks, bonds, real estate, or mutual funds, and choose investments that align with their risk tolerance and financial goals. By investing strategically and monitoring their investments regularly, business owners can grow their wealth and move closer to achieving their financial goals.

Lastly, seeking the guidance of a financial coach can be incredibly beneficial for business owners looking to achieve their financial goals. A financial coach can provide personalized guidance, accountability, and support to help business owners overcome financial challenges and make informed decisions. By collaborating with a financial coach, business owners can develop a clear financial plan, implement effective strategies, and stay motivated to achieve their financial goals.

Assessing the Financial Health of Your Business

Assessing the financial health of your business is crucial for ensuring its long-term success and sustainability. As a business owner, it is essential to regularly monitor and evaluate your company's financial performance to make informed decisions and identify areas for improvement. In this subchapter, we will discuss key aspects of assessing your business's economic health and provide practical tips on managing your finances effectively. One of the first steps in assessing your business's financial health is analyzing its financial statements. These documents, such as the income statement, balance sheet, and cash flow statement, provide valuable insights into your company's financial performance and overall health.

By reviewing these statements regularly, you can track your revenue, expenses, assets, and liabilities and identify any potential issues or discrepancies that need to be addressed. An aspect of assessing the financial health of your business is to calculate key financial ratios. These ratios, such as the current, quick, and debt-to-equity ratios, can help you evaluate your company's liquidity, solvency, and overall financial stability. By comparing these ratios to industry benchmarks and historical data, you can better understand how your business is performing and identify areas where improvements can be made.

Analyzing financial statements and calculating vital financial ratios is also essential, as is creating a budget and financial forecast for your business. A budget outlines your expected revenue and expenses for a specific period, while a financial forecast projects your company's financial performance over a longer time frame. Creating a budget and financial forecast allows you to set financial goals, track your progress, and make informed decisions to help your business grow and succeed.

Assessing the financial health of your business is vital for making informed decisions, identifying areas for improvement, and ensuring the long-term success of your company. By analyzing your financial statements, calculating vital financial ratios, and creating a budget and forecast, you can gain valuable insights into your business's financial performance and take initiative-taking steps to achieve your financial goals. Remember, financial fitness is not just about making money – it is about managing your finances effectively to build a strong and sustainable business.

Developing a Financial Plan

Developing a financial plan is essential for the success of any business. A financial plan is a roadmap that outlines a business's financial goals and strategies, helping to ensure that the company can achieve its objectives and remain financially stable. In this subchapter, we will discuss the critical components of developing a financial plan and provide insights into how business owners can effectively manage their finances with the help of financial coaching.

The first step in developing a financial plan is to set clear financial goals for the business. These goals should be specific, measurable, achievable, relevant, and time-bound (SMART). By setting SMART goals, business owners can create an unobstructed vision for their financial future and track their progress toward achieving these goals. Financial coaches can help business owners identify their financial goals and develop a plan to achieve them.

Once financial goals have been established, the next step is to create a budget that outlines the company's income and expenses. A well-developed budget is essential for tracking cash flow, managing expenses, and ensuring the business remains profitable. Financial coaches can assist business owners in creating a budget that aligns with their financial goals and helps them make informed decisions about their finances.

In addition to setting financial goals and creating a budget, business owners should also consider developing a savings plan and an investment strategy. A savings plan can help business owners build a financial cushion for unexpected expenses or emergencies, while an investment strategy can help them grow their wealth over time. Financial coaches can guide the best savings and investment options for business owners based on their financial goals and risk tolerance.

Finally, business owners should regularly review and update their financial plans to remain relevant and practical. By revisiting their financial goals, budget, savings plan, and investment strategy regularly, business owners can adjust as needed to stay on track toward achieving their financial objectives. Financial coaches can help business owners analyze their financial performance and make informed decisions about their finances to ensure long-term success for their businesses.

Implementing Cash Flow Management Strategies

Cash flow management is essential for the success of any business. It involves monitoring, analyzing, and optimizing the flow of money in and out of the company to ensure that there is enough cash on hand to meet financial obligations as they arise. Implementing cash flow management strategies is crucial for business owners to maintain economic stability and make informed decisions about their business operations.

One of the key strategies for effective cash flow management is creating a cash flow forecast. This involves projecting the business's future cash inflows and outflows based on historical data and current trends. By accurately predicting cash flow, business owners can anticipate potential cash shortages and take proactive steps to address them, such as securing financing or adjusting expenses.

Another important aspect of cash flow management is monitoring and controlling expenses. Business owners should regularly review their expenses and identify areas where costs can be reduced or eliminated. By cutting unnecessary expenses and negotiating better terms with suppliers, businesses can improve their cash flow and increase profitability.

It is also crucial for business owners to establish clear payment terms with customers and suppliers to ensure a steady flow of cash into the business. By setting payment terms that are favorable to the business, such as requiring upfront payments or offering discounts for advance payment, business owners can improve their cash flow and reduce the risk of overdue payments.

Business owners should consider implementing technology solutions to streamline their cash flow management processes. Various software tools are available that can automate invoicing, track expenses, and generate cash flow reports. By leveraging technology, business owners can save time and ensure greater accuracy in managing their cash flow, leading to improved financial health for the business.

Understanding Business Taxes

Understanding business taxes is crucial for any business owner, as taxes play a significant role in a company's financial health. Business taxes are different from personal taxes, as they are based on the income and expenses of the business itself. Business owners must clearly understand their tax obligations to avoid penalties and maximize their tax savings.

One key aspect of understanding business taxes is knowing what types of taxes your business is subject to. The most common types of business taxes include income, payroll, sales, and property taxes. Every kind of tax has its own set of rules and regulations, so it is essential to familiarize yourself with the specific requirements for each tax. Another important consideration regarding business taxes is keeping accurate and detailed records of all income and expenses. This includes tracking all revenue generated by the business and any deductions or credits that may apply. By maintaining organized and up-to-date financial records, you can ensure you correctly report your income and expenses to the IRS.

One way to minimize your business tax liability is to take advantage of tax deductions and credits that may be available. These can include deductions for business expenses such as rent, utilities, and supplies and credits for things like hiring veterans or investing in renewable energy. By collaborating with a financial coach or tax professional, you can identify potential tax savings opportunities and ensure you take full advantage of them. Understanding business taxes is a crucial aspect of running a successful business. By familiarizing yourself with the diverse types of taxes your company is subject to, keeping accurate financial records, and taking advantage of tax deductions and credits, you can minimize your tax liability and optimize your financial performance. Collaborating with a financial coach can help you navigate the complexities of business taxes and ensure you follow all relevant tax laws and regulations.

Tax Planning Strategies for Business Owners

Tax planning is an essential aspect of monetary management for business owners. Business owners can minimize their tax liability and maximize their profits by implementing effective tax planning strategies. In this subchapter, we will discuss some key tax planning strategies that can help business owners optimize their tax situation and achieve their financial goals.

One crucial tax planning strategy for business owners is to take advantage of tax deductions and credits that are available to them. By carefully tracking and documenting business expenses, business owners can reduce their taxable income and lower their overall tax bill. This can include deductions for items such as office supplies, travel expenses, and business insurance premiums. Additionally, business owners should be aware of any tax credits that may be available to them, such as the research and development credit or the small business health care tax credit. Another tax planning strategy for business owners is to structure their business in a tax-efficient manner. This may involve choosing the proper legal structure for the business, such as a sole proprietorship, partnership, or corporation. Each type of business structure has different tax implications, so business owners need to consult with a tax professional to determine the most advantageous structure for their specific situation.

Business owners should consider implementing tax-saving strategies such as income splitting, where income is distributed among family members in lower tax brackets. Business owners should also take the initiative to manage their tax liabilities throughout the year rather than wait until tax season to address tax issues. By regularly reviewing financial statements, monitoring cash flow, and staying up to date on changes in tax laws, business owners can identify tax planning opportunities and make informed decisions that can help reduce their tax burden. This proactive approach can also help business owners avoid costly tax penalties and interest charges.

Tax planning is a crucial component of financial fitness for business owners. Business owners can minimize their tax liability, optimize their economic situation, and achieve their long-term financial goals by implementing effective tax planning strategies. By staying informed, seeking professional advice, and taking an initiative-taking approach to tax planning, business owners can ensure that they make the most of their financial resources and build a solid foundation for future success.

Staying Compliant with Tax Laws

Staying compliant with tax laws is crucial for business owners to avoid penalties and legal issues. As a financial coach, it is essential to educate your clients on the importance of following tax regulations to maintain their businesses' financial health. By staying current on tax laws and regulations, business owners can ensure they meet their obligations and avoid costly mistakes.

One way to help business owners comply with tax laws is to encourage them to keep accurate and organized financial records. By maintaining detailed records of income, expenses, and deductions, business owners can easily track their tax liabilities and ensure they report their income correctly. This can help prevent errors on tax returns and reduce the risk of audits or penalties from tax authorities.

Another critical aspect of staying compliant with tax laws is understanding the deductions and credits available to business owners. As a financial coach, you can help your clients identify potential tax incentives that can help reduce their tax burden and maximize their savings. Business owners can lower their taxable income and keep more of their hard-earned money by taking advantage of available deductions and credits.

It is also important for business owners to stay informed about changes in tax laws that may affect their businesses. Tax regulations constantly evolve, and business owners must stay current on any updates or revisions that may impact their tax liability. By staying informed and seeking professional advice, business owners can ensure that they comply with all applicable tax laws and regulations.

Staying compliant with tax laws is a critical aspect of financial fitness for business owners. By keeping accurate records, understanding available deductions and credits, and staying informed about changes in tax laws, business owners can protect their businesses and avoid costly mistakes. As a financial coach, it is your role to educate and support your clients in maintaining compliance with tax regulations to ensure the long-term success of their businesses.

Types of Investments for Business Owners

When it comes to growing a business, one of the keys to success is making smart investments. As a business owner, it is important to understand the diverse types of investments available to you and how they can benefit your bottom line. In this subchapter, we will explore some of the most common types of investments for business owners.

One of the most popular types of investments for business owners is stocks. Investing in stocks allows you to own a small piece of a company and benefit from its growth and success. While stocks can be volatile, they also have the potential for high returns. Researching and carefully selecting the stocks you invest in to minimize risk and maximize potential gains is important. Another common investment option for business owners is real estate. Real estate can provide a steady stream of passive income through rental properties or the potential for significant returns through property appreciation. However, real estate investments come with their own set of risks and challenges, so it is important to do thorough due diligence before making any purchases.

Bonds can be a promising investment option for business owners looking for more stable and predictable returns. Bonds are loans made to governments or corporations that pay a fixed interest rate over a set period. While bonds typically offer lower returns than stocks, they also come with lower risk, making them a good option for conservative investors. I have found that business owners can also consider investing in mutual funds or exchange-traded funds (ETFs). These funds pool money from multiple investors to invest in a diversified portfolio of stocks, bonds, or other securities. This diversification helps spread risk and can provide more stable returns over the long term. Mutual funds and ETFs can be a good option for business owners who want to invest in the market but do not have the time or expertise to manage their portfolios.

Many more types of investments are available to business owners, each with its own set of risks and potential rewards. By understanding the options and doing thorough research, business owners can make smart investment decisions that help grow their businesses and secure their financial futures.

Risk Management and Diversification

Risk management and diversification are key concepts every business owner should understand and implement in their financial strategy. By managing risk and diversifying investments, business owners can protect their assets and ensure long-term financial stability.

One primary way to manage risk in business is through insurance. Business owners should have adequate insurance coverage to protect against unforeseen events such as natural disasters, accidents, or lawsuits. Business owners can mitigate potential financial losses and safeguard their assets by having the right insurance policies in place. Diversification is another important aspect of risk management. By spreading investments across different asset classes, industries, and geographic regions, business owners can reduce the impact of market volatility on their overall portfolio. Diversification helps lower the risk of significant losses and potentially increase returns over the long term.

Traditional investments such as stocks and bonds, business owners should also consider alternative investment options to further diversify their portfolio. These may include real estate, commodities, or private equity investments. Business owners can achieve a more balanced and resilient investment portfolio by diversifying across different asset classes.

Overall, risk management and diversification are essential components of a sound financial strategy for business owners. Business owners can protect their assets and ensure long-term financial success by managing risk through insurance and diversifying investments across different asset classes, industries, and regions. Business owners need to work with a financial coach to develop a comprehensive risk management and diversification strategy tailored to their specific needs and goals.

Working with Financial Advisors

Collaborating with financial advisors is essential for business owners seeking financial success and stability. These professionals are trained to provide expert advice on managing and growing your finances effectively. Business owners can gain valuable insights and strategies to optimize their monetary management practices by partnering with a financial advisor.

> A key benefit of working with a financial advisor is their ability to help business owners create a comprehensive financial plan. This plan can include short-term and long-term goals and strategies for achieving them. Financial advisors can also guide you on how to manage cash flow, reduce debt, and invest wisely. By collaborating closely with a financial advisor, business owners can develop a customized plan that aligns with their unique financial goals and objectives.

Financial advisors can also help business owners navigate complex financial decisions by creating a financial plan. Whether deciding on retirement plans, insurance coverage, or investment opportunities, a financial advisor can offer valuable insights and recommendations. By leveraging their expertise, business owners can make informed decisions that benefit their financial future.

Another important aspect of collaborating with financial advisors is their ability to provide ongoing support and guidance. As business owners' financial situations evolve, their advisors can help them adjust their strategies and make necessary changes. By maintaining a close relationship with their financial advisor, business owners can stay on track with their financial goals and adapt to changing market conditions.

Collaborating with a financial advisor can be a meaningful change for business owners seeking to improve their financial fitness. By leveraging their expertise, guidance, and support, business owners can make smarter financial decisions, achieve their goals, and secure their financial future. It is important for business owners to carefully select a financial advisor who aligns with their values, goals, and communication style to ensure a successful and beneficial partnership.

Recommended Books and Websites for Business Owners

As a business owner, it is essential to continuously educate yourself on financial fitness and management to ensure the success and growth of your business. In this subchapter, we will explore some recommended books and websites that can provide valuable insights and resources for business owners looking to improve their financial acumen.

One highly recommended book for business owners is "Profit First" by Mike Michalowicz. This book offers a revolutionary approach to managing your business finances by focusing on allocating profits first, rather than waiting until the end of the year to see what is left. It provides practical strategies and actionable steps to help you achieve financial stability and profitability in your business.

Another must-read book for business owners is "The E-Myth Revisited" by Michael E. Gerber. This book delves into the myths and misconceptions that many business owners have about running a successful business. It offers valuable insights on how to build a scalable and sustainable business model, as well as tips for effectively managing your time, resources, and finances. In addition to books, there are several websites that offer valuable resources and tools for business owners seeking financial coaching. One such website is the Small Business Administration (SBA) website, which provides a wealth of information on economic management, business planning, and access to funding resources. The SBA website also offers free online courses, webinars, and tools to help you improve your financial literacy and make informed decisions for your business.

Lastly, for business owners looking to stay updated on the latest trends and developments in financial coaching, websites like Entrepreneur, Forbes, and Inc. are invaluable resources. These websites feature articles, case studies, and expert insights from industry professionals that can help you stay ahead of the curve and make informed decisions for your business. By regularly exploring these recommended books and websites, business owners can enhance their financial fitness and achieve long-term success in their entrepreneurial endeavors.

Finding a Financial Coach

Finding the right financial coach for your business is a crucial step toward achieving financial success and stability. A financial coach can provide you with the guidance and expertise needed to navigate the complex world of business finances. In this subchapter, we will discuss the key considerations to keep in mind when looking for a financial coach that suits your needs and goals.

The first step in finding a financial coach is to assess your own financial situation and goals. Consider what areas of your business finances you need help with and what specific goals you want to achieve. This will help you narrow down your search for a financial coach who has expertise in those areas and can help you reach your goals effectively.

Once you have a clear understanding of your own financial needs and goals, it is time to start looking for a financial coach. You can ask for recommendations from other business owners, search online for financial coaches in your area, or attend financial coaching events and workshops to network with potential coaches. It is important to take the time to research and interview multiple coaches to find the right fit for you and your business.

When interviewing potential financial coaches, be sure to ask about their experience, qualifications, and approach to financial coaching. It is important to find a coach who has a solid track record of helping businesses like yours achieve financial success. Look for a coach who is knowledgeable, approachable, and able to communicate complex financial concepts in a way that is easy to understand. Finding the right financial coach for your business is a crucial step toward achieving your financial goals. By assessing your own financial situation and goals, conducting thorough research, and interviewing multiple coaches, you can find a financial coach who can provide you with the guidance and expertise needed to take your business to the next level financially.

Networking with Other Business Owners for Financial Support

Networking with other business owners for financial support can be a valuable strategy for businesses looking to secure funding or investment for their ventures. By building relationships with other entrepreneurs with successful businesses or access to capital, you can tap into a valuable network of resources and advice to help you achieve your financial goals.

One way to network with other business owners for financial support is to attend networking events and conferences to meet potential investors or partners. These events provide a valuable opportunity to connect with like-minded individuals who may be interested in financially supporting your business. Engaging in conversations and building relationships with other business owners can increase your chances of finding the financial support you need.

Another effective way to network with other business owners for financial support is to join industry-specific organizations or groups where you can connect with individuals who have experience in your field. These organizations often provide networking opportunities, mentorship programs, and access to resources that can help you secure funding for your business. By becoming an active member of these groups, you can build relationships with other business owners who can provide financial support or valuable advice.

In addition to attending events and joining industry organizations, leveraging social media and online platforms can be an effective way to network with other business owners for financial support. By connecting with other entrepreneurs on platforms like LinkedIn or Twitter, you can expand your network and potentially find individuals interested in investing in your business. Building an online presence and engaging with other business owners through social media can help you establish credibility and attract potential financial supporters.

Networking with other business owners for financial support is a valuable strategy for business owners looking to secure funding or investment for their ventures. By attending networking events, joining industry organizations, and leveraging social media, you can build relationships with other entrepreneurs who may be able to provide the financial support and guidance you need to succeed. By actively engaging in networking opportunities, you can expand your network, access valuable resources, and increase your chances of achieving your financial goals as a business owner.

Reflecting on Your Financial Journey

When it comes to managing your finances as a business owner, it is important to take the time to reflect on your financial journey. This can help you understand where you started, how far you have come, and where you want to go in the future. Reflecting on your financial journey can provide valuable insights and help you make informed decisions about your business finances.

One way to reflect on your financial journey is to review your financial goals and objectives. Take some time to revisit the goals you set when you started your business and assess whether you have achieved them. If you have not, think about what steps you can take to get back on track. It is important to regularly review and update your financial goals to ensure that they align with the current needs and priorities of your business.

Another important aspect of reflecting on your financial journey is to assess your current financial situation. Take a close look at your income, expenses, and cash flow to understand where your business stands financially. Are you making a profit, or are you struggling to break even? Identifying areas of financial strength and weakness can help you make strategic decisions to improve your financial health.

Regarding your goals and current financial situation, it is also important to consider any challenges or obstacles you have faced. Reflect on the lessons you have learned from these challenges and how they have shaped your financial decisions. By acknowledging and learning from your past experiences, you can better prepare for future financial challenges and opportunities. Overall, reflecting on your financial journey as a business owner is essential for building a solid financial foundation for your business. By assessing your goals, financial situation, and past experiences, you can gain valuable insights that will help you make informed decisions and achieve financial success. Remember, financial fitness is a journey, not a destination, so continue to reflect on your financial progress and adjust as needed to ensure the long-term financial health of your business.

Committing to Financial Fitness for the Long Run

Committing to Financial Fitness for the Long Run is essential for business owners who want to achieve long-term success and stability in their financial lives. To maintain a healthy financial situation, it is crucial to establish good habits and practices that will benefit your business eventually. This subchapter will provide valuable insights and strategies for business owners to improve their financial fitness and achieve their financial goals.

One key aspect of committing to financial fitness is creating a solid financial plan. This plan should outline your financial goals, budgeting strategies, investment strategies, and debt management. By creating a comprehensive financial plan, you can have a clear roadmap for your financial future and make informed decisions that will benefit your business eventually.

Another important aspect of committing to financial fitness is staying organized and disciplined in your financial practices. This includes keeping accurate records of your income and expenses, monitoring your cash flow, and regularly reviewing your financial statements. By staying organized and disciplined, you can identify any financial issues early on and take proactive steps to address them before they become major problems. Business owners should prioritize building an emergency fund to protect their business from unexpected financial setbacks. An emergency fund can provide a financial cushion in times of need and help you avoid taking on unnecessary debt to cover unexpected expenses. By building an emergency fund, you can ensure that your business remains financially stable and secure overall.

Committing to financial fitness also involves seeking guidance and support from a financial coach or advisor. A financial coach can provide valuable insights, guidance, and strategies to help you improve your financial fitness and achieve your financial goals. By working with a financial coach, you can gain a better understanding of your financial situation, identify areas for improvement, and develop a personalized plan to achieve your financial goals.

The Future of Financial Coaching for Business Owners

As we look towards the future of financial coaching for business owners, this industry is on the brink of significant growth and evolution. With the increasing complexity of financial markets and the ever-changing landscape of business ownership, the need for expert guidance in managing finances has never been greater. As technology continues to advance, we can expect to see more tools and resources available to financial coaches and their clients, allowing for more personalized and efficient financial planning strategies.

One of the key trends we can expect to see in the future of financial coaching for business owners is the integration of artificial intelligence and machine learning algorithms into financial planning processes. These technologies have the potential to revolutionize the way financial coaches analyze data, identify trends, and make recommendations to their clients. By harnessing the power of AI, financial coaches will be able to provide more accurate and timely financial advice, helping business owners make better-informed decisions about their finances.

Another important aspect of the future of financial coaching for business owners is the increasing focus on sustainability and social responsibility. As businesses become more aware of the impact their operations have on the environment and society, they are looking for financial coaches who can help them align their financial goals with their values. This shift towards sustainable and socially responsible investment will require financial coaches to stay informed about the latest trends and best practices in this area, to provide the most relevant and effective advice to their clients.

These technological and ethical considerations, the future of financial coaching for business owners will also be shaped by changing demographics and economic trends. As the workforce becomes increasingly diverse and globalized, financial coaches will need to adapt their strategies to meet the needs of a more diverse clientele. Additionally, as the economy continues to fluctuate and evolve, financial coaches will need to stay informed about the latest economic trends and market developments to provide the most accurate and relevant financial advice to their clients.

The future of financial coaching for business owners is bright and full of exciting opportunities for growth and innovation. By embracing modern technologies, focusing on sustainability and social responsibility, and staying informed about changing demographics and economic trends, financial coaches can position themselves as trusted advisors and valuable resources for business owners seeking to achieve financial success.

As we look towards the future, the role of the financial coach will only become more important and indispensable in helping business owners navigate the complexities of the financial world.

Challenging Your Inner Critic - Questioning the Inner Critic's Authority

Have you ever stopped to think about who put your inner critic in charge? I mean, who gave them the authority to berate you with negative self-talk constantly? Did you sign some contract in your sleep that we do not know about? It is time to start questioning the inner critic's authority and regain control of your self-esteem.

Let us face it: your inner critic is like that annoying friend who never has anything nice to say. They are constantly in your ear, pointing out all your flaws and mistakes. But who made them the judge and jury of your self-worth? Last time I checked, they didn't have a law degree or a PhD in psychology. So why are we letting them dictate how we feel about ourselves?

It's time to call out your inner critic for the fraud that they are. Next time they start spouting off negative self-talk, ask them for their credentials. I'm willing to bet they won't have much to say. And if they do, just remind yourself that they're probably just projecting their own insecurities onto you. So, take their criticism with a grain of salt (or a whole shaker, if you prefer).

Remember, your inner critic is like that annoying co-worker who always has something negative to say. But just because they're loud doesn't mean they're right. So, start questioning their authority and standing up for yourself. You deserve to be your own biggest cheerleader, not your own worst critic. It's time to silence the inner critic and take back control of your self-esteem. Start questioning their authority and reminding yourself that you oversee your own self-worth. So next time they try to bring you down with their negative self-talk, just tell them to take a hike. After all, who needs a critic when you can be your own biggest fan?

Cognitive Behavioural Techniques for Combatting Negative Self-Talk

Are you tired of hearing that pesky voice in your head constantly putting you down? Well, fear not, because it's time to silence that inner critic once and for all! In this subchapter, we will explore some cognitive behavioural techniques that will help you combat negative self-talk and finally give that voice a much-needed vacation.

First up, we have the classic technique of cognitive restructuring. This involves identifying the negative thoughts that pop into your head and replacing them with more positive and rational ones. For example, instead of thinking "I'm a failure," try replacing it with "I may have made a mistake, but that doesn't define my worth." It's like giving your inner critic a taste of its own medicine!

Next, we have the technique of behavioural experiments. This involves testing out your negative beliefs to see if they are true. For example, if you believe you are terrible at public speaking, try giving a speech in front of a small group of friends or family. You may just surprise yourself and realize that you're not as bad as you thought! Another fun technique to try is thought stopping. This involves literally shouting "STOP!" in your head whenever a negative thought creeps in. It's a simple yet effective way to interrupt that inner critic's constant chatter and give yourself a moment of peace and quiet.

And let's not forget about the power of humour in combatting negative self-talk. Sometimes, the best way to silence that inner critic is to make fun of it. Imagine that voice as a cartoon character with a silly voice or give it a ridiculous name like "Negative Nelly." By poking fun at your inner critic, you take away its power and remind yourself that those negative thoughts are just that – thoughts, not truths.

So, there you have it, a few cognitive behavioural techniques to help you combat negative self-talk and finally silence that pesky inner critic. Remember, you are in control of your thoughts, not the other way around. So go ahead, give these techniques a try and show that inner critic who's boss!

Building Self-Compassion and Self-Esteem

Welcome to the subchapter on building self-compassion and self-esteem! If you've ever found yourself caught in a never-ending cycle of negative self-talk, you're not alone. We all have that little voice in our heads that loves to point out our flaws and shortcomings. But fear not, dear adults, for we are here to help you silence that pesky inner critic once and for all.

First and foremost, it's important to remember that you are your own worst critic. Seriously, if we talked to our friends the way we talk to ourselves, we'd have zero friends left. So, let's cut ourselves some slack and start practicing self-compassion. Treat yourself like you would treat your best friend - with kindness, understanding, and a healthy dose of humour. After all, laughter is the best medicine for silencing that inner critic.

Next up, let's tackle the issue of self-esteem. It's time to stop comparing ourselves to others and start embracing our unique qualities and quirks. So, what if you can't bake a perfect souffle or run a marathon in record time? Embrace your imperfections and celebrate your accomplishments, no matter how big or small. Remember, you are enough just as you are, flaws and all.

One great way to boost your self-esteem is to practice positive affirmations. Repeat after me: "I am awesome. I am worthy. I am capable of achieving great things." Say it loud, say it proud, and start believing in yourself. You've got this, adults! And if all else fails, just remember that Beyonce wasn't built in a day. It takes time and effort to build self-esteem, but with a little bit of humour and a whole lot of self-love, you can conquer that inner critic once and for all.

So, go forth and practice self-compassion, embrace your uniqueness, and boost your self-esteem like the badass adults you are. Remember, you are the master of your own thoughts, so don't let that inner critic bully you into submission. Silencing the inner critic is a journey, not a destination, so buckle up and enjoy the ride. And hey, if all else fails, just remember that you're not alone in this struggle. We're all in this together, so let's support each other in overcoming self-limiting beliefs and negative self-talk. Cheers to building self-compassion and self-esteem!

LESSON

5

Sustainability Leads to Resilience

Resilience In the Long run

In cultivating trust in God's plan, we must also remember that His timing is perfect. It can be easy to become impatient or discouraged when things do not go according to our own plans, but we must trust that God's timing is always right. By surrendering our own timelines and agendas, we can align ourselves with God's will and find peace in knowing that He is working all things together for our good.

> "Success is not a mere dream, it is a tangible reality waiting to be achieved. Don't just dream of success, take action and make it happen."
>
> – ETHAN R. ESBACH

Self-care Practices for Business Owners

As a business owner, it is crucial to prioritize self-care practices to maintain a resilient mindset and overcome the challenges that come with running a business. Self-care is not just about pampering yourself, but rather about taking the time to prioritize your physical, mental, and emotional well-being to function at your best. In this subchapter, we will explore some self-care practices that can help business owners build resilience and navigate the ups and downs of entrepreneurship.

One important self-care practice for business owners is setting boundaries. It can be easy to let work consume your life, but it is essential to establish clear boundaries between work and personal time. This means setting specific work hours, unplugging from technology when you are not working, and making time for activities that bring you joy and relaxation. By setting boundaries, you can prevent burnout and maintain a healthy work-life balance.

Another self-care practice for business owners is practicing mindfulness. Mindfulness involves being present in the moment and paying attention to your thoughts and feelings without judgment. By practicing mindfulness, you can reduce stress, improve focus, and enhance your overall well-being. Taking a few minutes each day to practice mindfulness through activities such as meditation, deep breathing, or simply taking a walk can have a significant impact on your resilience and ability to overcome challenges.

Exercise is another important self-care practice for business owners. Regular physical activity has been shown to reduce stress, improve mood, and boost energy levels. Whether it's going for a run, practicing yoga, or hitting the gym, finding time to move your body can help you build resilience and stay healthy. Make exercise a priority in your schedule and notice the positive effects it has on your mindset and ability to handle challenges.

By setting boundaries, practicing mindfulness, and exercising, it is important for business owners to prioritize self-care through healthy eating and sleep habits. Eating a balanced diet rich in fruits, vegetables, lean proteins, and whole grains can provide your body with the nutrients it needs to function optimally. Additionally, getting an adequate amount of sleep each night is crucial for maintaining a resilient mindset and managing stress. By taking care of your physical health through proper nutrition and sleep, you can better equip yourself to handle the demands of running a business and bounce back from setbacks with resilience.

Setting Boundaries and Prioritizing Well-being

Setting boundaries and prioritizing well-being are crucial aspects of maintaining a resilient mindset in the business world. As business owners, it is easy to get caught up in the hustle and bustle of day-to-day operations, but neglecting our personal well-being can have detrimental effects on our overall success. By setting boundaries and making self-care a priority, we can not only improve our mental and physical health but also enhance our productivity and decision-making abilities.

SUSTAINABILITY LEADS TO RESILIENCE

One of the first steps in setting boundaries is learning to say no. As business owners, we are often bombarded with requests and opportunities that can easily overwhelm us if we try to take on too much. By learning to say no to things that do not align with our goals or values, we can free up time and energy to focus on what truly matters. This can help prevent burnout and ensure that we are able to give our best to the tasks and projects that are most important to us.

Another important aspect of setting boundaries is establishing clear expectations with clients, employees, and partners. By communicating our needs and limitations upfront, we can avoid misunderstandings and prevent resentment from building up over time. This can help create a more positive and productive work environment, where everyone feels respected and valued. It is important to remember that setting boundaries is not a sign of weakness, but rather a sign of self-awareness and self-respect.

> Prioritizing well-being also involves taking care of ourselves physically, mentally, and emotionally. This can include getting enough sleep, eating well, exercising regularly, and taking time for activities that bring us joy and relaxation. Making time for self-care can help reduce stress, improve our mood, and increase our resilience in the face of challenges. It is important to remember that taking care of ourselves is not selfish, but rather necessary for our long-term success and well-being. By setting boundaries and prioritizing well-being are essential for maintaining a resilient mindset in the business world.

By learning to say no, establishing clear expectations, and taking care of ourselves, we can improve our mental and physical health, enhance our productivity, and build stronger relationships with those around us. As business owners, it is important to remember that our well-being is not a luxury, but a necessity for thriving in both our personal and professional lives.

Celebrating Successes and Learning from Failures

As business owners, it is essential to celebrate our successes and learn from our failures to maintain a resilient mindset. Celebrating successes helps us to acknowledge our hard work and accomplishments, boosting our morale and motivation to continue striving for excellence. It is important to take the time to reflect on our achievements and recognize the progress we have made in our personal growth and development.

On the other hand, learning from our failures is equally important in building resilience. Failure is a natural part of the entrepreneurial journey, and it provides valuable lessons that can help us grow and improve. By analysing our failures and understanding the reasons behind them, we can identify areas for improvement and make necessary adjustments to our strategies. Embracing failure as a learning opportunity can ultimately lead to greater success in the long run.

One way to celebrate successes and learn from failures is through regular reflection and self-assessment. Take the time to review your goals, accomplishments, and setbacks on a regular basis. Celebrate your wins, no matter how small, and use them as motivation to keep pushing forward. Likewise, analyse your failures objectively and identify the lessons learned that can be applied to future endeavours. Another important aspect of celebrating successes and learning from failures is to share your experiences with others. By sharing your successes, you can inspire and motivate others in their own journeys towards personal growth and development. Similarly, sharing your failures can help others learn from your mistakes and avoid similar pitfalls. Building a community of support and learning from each other's experiences can strengthen resilience and foster a culture of continuous improvement.

Celebrating successes and learning from failures are integral components of maintaining a resilient mindset in business. By taking the time to acknowledge our achievements and reflect on our setbacks, we can continue to grow and develop both personally and professionally. Embracing both the highs and lows of entrepreneurship can help us build resilience, learn valuable lessons, and ultimately achieve greater success in our endeavours.

Resilience as a Competitive Advantage

In the world of business, resilience is not just a personal quality, but a competitive advantage that can set you apart from your competitors. In today's fast-paced and constantly changing business landscape, the ability to bounce back from setbacks and adapt to new challenges is essential for success. As a business owner, developing a resilient mindset can help you navigate the ups and downs of entrepreneurship with grace and confidence.

Resilience in personal growth and development is about more than just being able to weather storms – it's about thriving in the face of adversity. When you cultivate a resilient mindset, you are better equipped to handle stress, overcome obstacles, and persevere in the face of uncertainty. This not only benefits your own well-being, but also has a positive impact on your business. By modelling resilience for your employees and stakeholders, you create a culture of strength and perseverance that can help your company weather any storm.

One of the key components of resilience in business is the ability to adapt to change. In today's rapidly evolving marketplace, businesses that can pivot and innovate in response to new challenges are the ones that thrive. By cultivating a resilient mindset, you can approach change with a sense of curiosity and openness, rather than fear and resistance. This allows you to embrace new opportunities and pivot your business strategy as needed to stay ahead of the competition. Another important aspect of resilience in business is the ability to bounce back from failure. In the world of entrepreneurship, setbacks and failures are inevitable – but it's how you respond to them that matters. By developing a resilient mindset, you can view failure as a learning opportunity rather than a defeat. This allows you to bounce back stronger and more determined than before, ready to tackle whatever challenges come your way.

Resilience in business is about building a foundation of strength and adaptability that allows you to thrive in the face of adversity. By cultivating a resilient mindset, you can not only overcome challenges, but also turn them into opportunities for growth and success. As a business owner, developing a resilient mindset is one of the most powerful tools you have at your disposal – one that can help you build a thriving business that can weather any storm.

Leveraging Challenges for Growth and Innovation

In the world of business, challenges and obstacles are inevitable. As business owners, it is crucial to have a resilient mindset to overcome these hurdles and continue to grow and innovate. By leveraging these challenges, we can not only survive in the competitive market but also thrive and reach new heights of success. One of the keyways to leverage challenges for growth and innovation is to view them as opportunities for learning and improvement. Instead of being discouraged by setbacks, see them as valuable lessons that can help you refine your strategies and make better decisions in the future. Embrace the mindset of continuous improvement and use every challenge as a chance to strengthen your skills and knowledge.

Another way to leverage challenges is to seek out innovative solutions that can turn obstacles into advantages. Think outside the box and explore new ideas and technologies that can help you overcome obstacles in creative ways. By being open to change and innovation, you can transform challenges into opportunities for growth and development. It is also important to stay resilient in the face of adversity. Develop a strong support system of mentors, colleagues, and friends who can provide guidance and encouragement during tough times. Surround yourself with positive influences and stay focused on your goals, even when faced with setbacks. By cultivating a resilient mindset, you can bounce back from challenges stronger and more determined than ever before.

I have found that leveraging challenges for growth and innovation is essential for business owners who want to succeed in today's competitive market. By viewing obstacles as opportunities for learning, seeking out innovative solutions, and staying resilient in the face of adversity, you can turn challenges into stepping stones for success. Embrace the mindset of resilience and see every challenge as a chance to grow and thrive in your personal and professional development.

Inspiring Resilience in Others

In the competitive world of business, resilience is a key trait that can make or break a business owner. It is the ability to bounce back from setbacks, adapt to change, and persevere in the face of challenges. As a business owner, it is important to not only cultivate your own resilience but also inspire resilience in others. By fostering a culture of resilience within your team, you can create a more productive and successful business environment.

One way to inspire resilience in others is by leading by example. Show your team that you can overcome challenges and setbacks with a positive attitude and determination. Share your own stories of resilience and how you were able to overcome obstacles in your business journey. By showing vulnerability and authenticity, you can inspire others to do the same and develop their own resilience.

Another way to inspire resilience in others is by providing support and encouragement. Let your team know that you believe in their abilities and that you are there to support them through difficult times. Encourage open communication and create a safe space for team members to share their struggles and seek help when needed. By providing a supportive environment, you can help your team build their resilience and overcome obstacles together.

It is also important to empower your team members to take ownership of their own resilience. Encourage them to set goals, develop action plans, and take proactive steps to overcome challenges. Provide them with the resources and tools they need to succeed and give them the autonomy to make decisions and take risks. By empowering your team members to take control of their own resilience, you can help them develop the skills and mindset needed to overcome any obstacle that comes their way.

Lastly, celebrate and recognize resilience in your team members. Acknowledge their efforts and achievements, no matter how small, and show appreciation for their resilience in the face of adversity. By highlighting and celebrating resilience, you can reinforce this important trait within your team and inspire others to develop their own resilience. By fostering a culture of resilience within your business, you can create a more resilient and successful team that is able to overcome any challenge that comes their way. One other thing to know is that Christian resilience have its key elements

The Importance of Resilience in Church Leadership

In the world of church leadership, resilience is a crucial quality that can make all the difference in the success of a ministry. The ability to bounce back from setbacks, navigate challenges with grace, and maintain a steadfast faith in the face of adversity is essential for those who are called to lead God's people. In this subchapter, we will explore the importance of resilience in church leadership and how strengthening our foundations in faith can help us weather the storms that inevitably come our way.

One of the key reasons why resilience is so important in church leadership is the fact that the work of ministry can be incredibly demanding and draining. Leaders are often called upon to provide support and guidance to those who are struggling, deal with difficult personalities and conflicts within the congregation, and navigate the challenges of managing a non-profit organization. Without resilience, it can be all too easy to become overwhelmed and burnt out. By cultivating a spirit of resilience, church leaders can better cope with the pressures of their roles and continue to serve with joy and passion.

Additionally, resilience is essential for weathering the inevitable storms that come our way in ministry. Whether it is the sudden loss of a key staff member, a financial crisis, or a conflict within the congregation, church leaders must be able to navigate these challenges with grace and faith. By strengthening our foundations in faith and building our resilience, we can approach these challenges with confidence, knowing that God is with us every step of the way.

Furthermore, resilience is important for setting a positive example for the congregation. As church leaders, we are called to be beacons of hope and faith for those we serve. By demonstrating resilience in the face of challenges, we can inspire others to do the same. Our ability to bounce back from setbacks and remain steadfast in our faith can encourage others to do likewise, creating a culture of resilience within the congregation.

The importance of resilience in church leadership cannot be overstated. By strengthening our foundations in faith and cultivating a spirit of resilience, we can better navigate the challenges of ministry, set a positive example for our congregations, and continue to serve with passion and joy. As we continue to grow in Christian spiritual resilience, we can be confident that God will sustain us through every trial and tribulation that comes our way.

Biblical Examples of Resilience

In times of uncertainty and adversity, it can be challenging to remain steadfast in our faith. However, as church leaders, it is crucial that we demonstrate resilience in the face of trials and tribulations. The Bible provides us with numerous examples of individuals who displayed unwavering faith and resilience during difficult circumstances. By studying these biblical examples, we can draw inspiration and strength to navigate the challenges that come our way.

> One powerful example of resilience in the Bible is the story of Job. Despite experiencing unimaginable loss and suffering, Job remained faithful to God. Through his unwavering trust in God, Job was able to endure his trials and experience restoration and blessings. Job's story serves as a reminder that even in our darkest moments, God is always present and faithful to see us through.

Another biblical example of resilience is found in the life of Joseph. Joseph endured betrayal, slavery, and imprisonment, yet he never wavered in his faith. Through unwavering trust in God's plan, Joseph was able to rise from a position of lowliness to become a powerful leader in Egypt. Joseph's story teaches us the importance of trusting in God's timing and remaining steadfast in our faith, even when circumstances seem bleak.

The story of David and Goliath is another powerful example of resilience in the Bible. Despite facing an insurmountable foe, David trusted in God's strength and was able to defeat Goliath with just a sling and a stone. David's courage and faith serve as a reminder that with God on our side, we can overcome any obstacle that stands in our way. By following David's example of boldness and trust in God, we can face our challenges with confidence and resilience.

As church leaders, it is essential that we cultivate resilience in our own lives and model it for those under our care. By studying the biblical examples of resilience, we can learn valuable lessons about trust, perseverance, and faith in the face of adversity. Let us draw strength from the stories of Job, Joseph, David, and countless others who have demonstrated unwavering faith in God. As we deepen our spiritual resilience, we will be better equipped to lead our churches and organizations through the challenges that lie ahead.

Defining Christian Spiritual Resilience

In today's world, where challenges and trials are ever-present, the concept of Christian spiritual resilience has become increasingly important for churches, church leadership, foundations, and non-profit organizations. But what exactly does it mean to have Christian spiritual resilience?

At its core, Christian spiritual resilience is the ability to bounce back from adversity, to stand firm in the face of trials, and to remain rooted in faith despite the storms of life. It is about drawing strength from God's Word, prayer, and community, and trusting in His plan even when things seem bleak. For churches and church leadership, cultivating Christian spiritual resilience is essential to navigate the complexities of ministry and to lead with grace and wisdom. It is about setting an example for others, showing them how to rely on God's strength and to persevere through difficulties with unwavering faith.

Foundations and non-profit organizations also play a crucial role in fostering Christian spiritual resilience within their communities. By providing support, resources, and a safe space for individuals to grow in their faith, these organizations can help strengthen the spiritual foundations of those they serve. Christian spiritual resilience is about recognizing that our strength comes from God alone. It is about embracing challenges as opportunities for growth and trusting that God will carry us through even the darkest of times. By building a solid foundation in faith and staying connected to a supportive community, we can weather any storm with confidence and hope.

Deepening Personal Relationship with God

Deepening our personal relationship with God is a crucial aspect of building Christian resilience. As church leaders, it is important for us to continually seek ways to strengthen our foundations in faith and grow closer to the Lord. By deepening our personal relationship with God, we are better equipped to manage the challenges and trials that come our way, and to lead our congregations with strength and conviction.

> One way to deepen our personal relationship with God is through regular prayer and meditation. Taking the time to communicate with God daily helps us to center ourselves and stay focused on His will for our lives. Through prayer, we can seek guidance, find comfort, and draw strength from the One who has promised to never leave us nor forsake us.

Another way to deepen our personal relationship with God is through studying His Word. The Bible is a source of wisdom, encouragement, and direction for our lives. By spending time in Scripture each day, we can learn more about God's character, His promises, and His plan for our lives. The more we immerse ourselves in God's Word, the more we will come to know and love Him.

Fellowship with other believers is also key to deepening our personal relationship with God. As church leaders, we need to surround ourselves with a strong community of faith. By sharing our struggles, victories, and experiences with other believers, we can encourage one another, hold each other accountable, and grow together in our walk with the Lord.

Deepening our relationship with God is essential for building Christian resilience and strengthening our foundations in faith. As church leaders, let us commit to seeking God through prayer, studying His Word, and fellowship with other believers. By doing so, we will be better equipped to face the challenges of ministry and lead with courage, wisdom, and grace.

Cultivating Trust in God's Plan

One of the key foundations we must cultivate in building spiritual resilience is trust in God's plan. As church leaders, we understand the challenges and uncertainties that come with leading a congregation or running a non-profit organization. It is in these moments of doubt and fear that we must lean on our faith and trust that God has a plan for us, even when we cannot see it clearly.

Trusting in God's plan does not mean that we will never face difficulties or hardships. In fact, it is often amid these challenges that our faith is tested and strengthened. By surrendering control and placing our trust in God, we can find peace and comfort knowing that He is guiding us every step of the way. This trust allows us to let go of our worries and fears, knowing that God's plan is greater than anything we could imagine.

As church leaders, it is important to model this trust in God's plan for our congregations and organizations. By sharing our own struggles and demonstrating how we rely on God's guidance, we can inspire others to do the same. Through transparency and vulnerability, we can build a community that supports each other in times of uncertainty and hardship, knowing that we are all part of God's greater plan.

> In cultivating trust in God's plan, we must also remember that His timing is perfect. It can be easy to become impatient or discouraged when things do not go according to our own plans, but we must trust that God's timing is always right. By surrendering our own timelines and agendas, we can align ourselves with God's will and find peace in knowing that He is working all things together for our good.

Trust in God's plan is essential to building spiritual resilience as church leaders. By surrendering control, trusting in God's guidance, and embracing His perfect timing, we can find strength and peace amid uncertainty. Let us continue to lean on our faith and trust that God's plan is greater than anything we could imagine, knowing that He is with us every step of the way.

Embracing Perseverance and Endurance

In the journey of faith and leadership, embracing perseverance and endurance is essential for building spiritual resilience. As church leaders, we are called to navigate through various challenges and obstacles that may come our way. It is through perseverance and endurance that we can strengthen our foundations in faith and continue to lead with courage and conviction.

Perseverance is the ability to persist in the face of adversity and setbacks. It is the determination to keep going even when things get tough. As church leaders, we must embody perseverance in our ministries, trusting in God's plan and His timing. By staying steadfast in our faith and refusing to give up, we can inspire those around us to do the same.

Endurance is the capacity to withstand hardships and difficulties without losing hope or faith. It is the resilience to keep moving forward, even when the road ahead seems long and challenging. As church leaders, we must cultivate endurance in our spiritual journey, knowing that God is with us every step of the way. By enduring through trials and tribulations, we can grow stronger in our faith and become a beacon of hope for others.

Together, perseverance and endurance form the bedrock of Christian spiritual resilience. They enable us to weather the storms of life and emerge stronger on the other side. As church leaders, we must embrace these qualities wholeheartedly, trusting in God's provision and his unfailing love. By leaning on Him for strength and guidance, we can navigate through any obstacle with grace and confidence.

May we, as church leaders, continue to cultivate perseverance and endurance in our ministries, knowing that God is our ultimate source of strength and hope. Let us press on with faith and determination, knowing that our efforts are not in vain. With God's help, we can overcome any challenge and emerge victorious, shining brightly as a testament to His grace and mercy.

Navigating Spiritual Warfare

Navigating Spiritual Warfare can be a challenging and daunting task for church leaders and organizations, but it is essential in building Christian resilience. As we face spiritual battles, it is important to remember that we are not alone in this fight. God is with us every step of the way, providing us with the strength and guidance we need to overcome any obstacles that come our way.

One key aspect of navigating spiritual warfare is staying rooted in prayer and scripture. By immersing ourselves in God's Word and communicating with Him through prayer, we can gain a deeper understanding of His will for our lives and the strength to face any trials that may come our way. Prayer is a powerful tool that can help us to connect with God and seek His guidance in times of need.

Another important aspect of navigating spiritual warfare is staying connected to a community of believers. Surrounding ourselves with fellow Christians who can offer support, encouragement, and prayer is essential in building Christian resilience. Together, we can stand firm in our faith and support one another as we face spiritual battles.

In addition to prayer and community, it is also important to equip ourselves with the armor of God. Ephesians 6:10-18 reminds us to put on the full armor of God, including the belt of truth, the breastplate of righteousness, the shield of faith, the helmet of salvation, and the sword of the Spirit. By putting on this armor, we can stand strong in the face of spiritual attacks and defend ourselves against the enemy.

Navigating spiritual warfare is not easy, but with God's strength and guidance, we can overcome any challenges that come our way. By staying rooted in prayer, connected to a community of believers, and equipped with the armor of God, we can build Christian resilience and stand firm in our faith. Let us continue to trust in God and rely on His power as we navigate the spiritual battles that come our way.

Dealing with Criticism and Opposition

In the journey of Christian leadership, one of the biggest challenges that we may face is criticism and opposition. It is inevitable that as we strive to fulfill God's calling on our lives, there will be those who do not understand or agree with our decisions and actions. However, it is important to remember that God is our ultimate judge, and His opinion of us is what truly matters. Therefore, when faced with criticism and opposition, we must turn to Him for strength and guidance.

When dealing with criticism and opposition, it is crucial to maintain a spirit of humility and openness. Instead of becoming defensive or argumentative, we should listen carefully to the concerns and feedback of others. By doing so, we can learn and grow from the perspectives of those who may see things differently than we do. In this way, we can turn what may seem like a negative experience into an opportunity for personal and spiritual growth. It is also important to remember that criticism and opposition can sometimes be a sign that we are on the right path. Jesus himself faced intense opposition during his ministry on earth, yet he remained steadfast in his mission to bring salvation to the world.

> As followers of Christ, we can take comfort in knowing that we are in good company when we encounter resistance in our own ministries. By staying true to our calling and trusting in God's plan, we can overcome any obstacles that come our way.

In times of criticism and opposition, it is essential to surround ourselves with a supportive community of fellow believers. By leaning on one another for encouragement and prayer, we can find strength and resilience to face the challenges that come our way. As church leaders, we must foster an environment of love and unity within our congregations, where we can support and uplift one another in times of difficulty. Together, we can weather any storm that comes our way, knowing that God is with us every step of the journey.

Ultimately, dealing with criticism and opposition is an opportunity for us to deepen our faith and trust in God. By remaining steadfast in our convictions and seeking His guidance in all that we do, we can overcome any obstacles that come our way. As church leaders, let us stand firm in our faith, knowing that God's strength is made perfect in our weaknesses. With God's help, we can navigate the challenges of criticism and opposition with grace and resilience, emerging stronger and more steadfast in our calling than ever before.

Finding Strength in Weakness

In times of struggle and adversity, it can be easy to feel overwhelmed and defeated. However, as Christian leaders, we must remember that our strength does not come from ourselves, but from God. It is in our weakness that we can find true strength, as the apostle Paul reminds us in 2 Corinthians 12:9-10: "But he said to me, 'My grace is sufficient for you, for my power is made perfect in weakness.' Therefore, I will boast more gladly about my weaknesses, so that Christ's power may rest on me. That is why, for Christ's sake, I delight in weaknesses, in insults, in hardships, in persecutions, in difficulties. For when I am weak, then I am strong."

When we embrace our weaknesses and rely on God's strength, we can experience a deep sense of peace and resilience that surpasses all understanding. As church leaders, we must lead by example and show others that it is okay to not have all the answers or to feel overwhelmed at times. By being vulnerable and transparent about our own struggles, we can create a safe space for others to do the same and find strength in their weakness.

It is important for us as church leaders to cultivate a culture of support and encouragement within our churches and organizations. We must remind ourselves and others that it is okay to lean on one another and to ask for help when needed. By coming together in times of weakness, we can strengthen our bonds as a community and grow in our faith together. During challenges and trials, we must remember that God is always with us, providing us with the strength and courage we need to persevere. It is through our faith and trust in Him that we can find the resilience to overcome any obstacle that comes our way. As church leaders, we must continually remind ourselves and our congregations of God's faithfulness and promise to never leave nor forsake us.

May we all find strength in our weaknesses and trust in God's unfailing love and power. Let us lean on one another and lift each other up in prayer, knowing that together we can weather any storm. With God as our foundation, we can stand firm in our faith and lead with courage and resilience in all that we do.

Creating a Supportive Environment for Leaders

Creating a supportive environment for leaders is crucial in fostering their spiritual resilience and ensuring their success in guiding their churches and nonprofit organizations. As leaders face numerous challenges and pressures in their roles, it is essential for them to have a dedicated support system in place. By building a supportive environment, we can help leaders thrive in their positions and continue to serve their communities with passion and dedication.

One way to create a supportive environment for leaders is to prioritize open communication and transparency within the organization. Leaders should feel comfortable sharing their struggles and concerns with their peers and mentors, as well as receiving feedback and guidance from others.

By fostering a culture of open communication, we can help leaders feel supported and valued in their roles, leading to increased resilience in the face of adversity.

In addition to open communication, it is important to provide leaders with opportunities for self-care and personal growth. Encouraging leaders to take time for themselves, practice self-care activities, and engage in spiritual practices can help them recharge and maintain their spiritual resilience. By investing in the well-being of our leaders, we can ensure that they have the strength and energy to lead effectively and positively impact their communities.

Moreover, creating a supportive environment for leaders involves promoting a culture of collaboration and teamwork. By encouraging leaders to work together, share resources, and support one another in their endeavors, we can foster a sense of unity and camaraderie within the organization. This sense of community can help leaders feel connected and supported, even during challenging times, strengthening their resilience and fortitude.

Creating a supportive environment for leaders is essential in promoting their spiritual resilience and ensuring their success in their roles. By prioritizing open communication, self-care, collaboration, and unity within the organization, we can help leaders thrive and continue to make a positive impact on their communities. Let us come together to support and uplift our leaders, so they can continue to serve with passion and dedication, strengthening the foundations of faith for generations to come.

Encouraging Vulnerability and Authenticity

To foster true spiritual resilience within our churches and organizations, it is crucial to encourage vulnerability and authenticity among our members and leaders. By creating a safe space for individuals to share their struggles, doubts, and fears, we allow for genuine connection and growth to take place. When we hide behind a facade of perfection, we deny ourselves the opportunity to experience the healing power of vulnerability and the strength that comes from authentic relationships.

It is important for church leadership to lead by example in this regard, demonstrating vulnerability and authenticity in their own lives. By sharing their own struggles and shortcomings, leaders can create a culture of openness and acceptance within the community. When we are willing to be vulnerable with one another, we show that it is safe to be imperfect and that we are all in need of God's grace and mercy.

Encouraging vulnerability and authenticity also allows for deeper spiritual growth and transformation to occur within our churches and organizations. When we are willing to confront our fears and insecurities, we open ourselves up to the work of the Holy Spirit in our lives. By being authentic about our struggles and weaknesses, we create space for God to work in and through us, leading to greater spiritual resilience and maturity.

In a world that often values image and success more than anything else, it can be challenging to embrace vulnerability and authenticity. However, as Christians, we are called to be counter-cultural in our approach to relationships and community. By encouraging vulnerability and authenticity within our churches and organizations, we can create a place where people feel truly seen, heard, and loved for who they are, not for who they pretend to be.

Let us strive to cultivate a culture of openness and honesty within our communities, where vulnerability is celebrated, and authenticity is valued. By embracing our imperfections and weaknesses, we can experience the transformative power of God's love and grace in our lives, leading to greater spiritual resilience and deeper connection with one another.

Promoting a Culture of Resilience in Churches

Promoting a culture of resilience in churches is essential for the spiritual well-being of both church leaders and members. Resilience allows individuals to bounce back from adversity, setbacks, and challenges with renewed strength and faith. By fostering a culture of resilience within the church community, leaders can empower their members to navigate life's difficulties with grace and trust in God's plan.

One way to promote a culture of resilience in churches is by emphasizing the importance of prayer and spiritual practices. Encouraging church members to lean on their faith during times of struggle can provide a sturdy foundation for resilience. By fostering a community that values prayer and spiritual growth, church leaders can help their members develop a deeper connection to God and find strength in times of need.

Another key aspect of promoting resilience in churches is fostering a sense of community and support among members. Church leaders can create opportunities for fellowship, connection, and mutual support within the congregation. By building strong relationships and a sense of belonging within the church community, members can feel supported and cared for during challenging times, strengthening their resilience and faith.

> An active prayer life, spiritual practices, and community support, church leaders can also promote resilience by providing resources and tools for personal growth and development. This can include offering workshops, seminars, and resources on topics such as stress management, emotional well-being, and building resilience. By equipping church members with the knowledge and skills to navigate life's challenges, leaders can help them cultivate a solid foundation of resilience.

In cultivating a culture of resilience within churches, leaders are not only strengthening the individual faith of their members but also building a solid foundation for the entire community. By promoting prayer, spiritual practices, community support, and personal growth, churches can empower their members to face life's challenges with courage, faith, and resilience. Through these efforts, church leaders can create a community that is strong, resilient, and deeply rooted in the foundation of Christian faith.

Practicing Self-Care and Emotional Wellness

Practicing self-care and emotional wellness is essential for maintaining resilience in the face of challenges and adversity. As church leaders, it can be easy to pour all our energy into serving others and neglect our own well-being. However, taking care of us is crucial for effectively ministering to others and fulfilling our calling with strength and grace.

One key aspect of self-care is setting boundaries and learning to say no when necessary. It is important to recognize our limitations and prioritize our own mental, emotional, and physical health. This may mean delegating tasks, taking breaks when needed, and seeking support from others. By valuing our own well-being, we are better equipped to serve others and fulfill our roles as church leaders but be mindful of setting boundaries, practicing self-care also involves nurturing our emotional wellness.

This can include engaging in activities that bring us joy, such as hobbies, exercise, or spending time with loved ones. It may also involve seeking professional help or therapy when needed to address any emotional struggles or trauma. By taking care of our emotional health, we can better navigate the difficulties of ministry and maintain a sturdy foundation in faith.

As church leaders, we are called to be a source of strength and support for others. However, it is important to remember that we are not immune to struggles and challenges ourselves. By prioritizing self-care and emotional wellness, we can better fulfill our calling and serve others with compassion and grace. Let us commit to taking care of ourselves so that we can continue to be a beacon of hope and resilience for those we serve.

Practicing self-care and emotional wellness is a vital aspect of maintaining resilience in our roles as church leaders. By setting boundaries, nurturing our emotional wellness, and prioritizing our own well-being, we can better serve others and fulfill our calling with strength and grace. Let us embrace self-care as a necessary component of our ministry and commit to taking care of ourselves so that we can continue to be a source of strength and support for those in need.

Seeking Accountability and Mentorship

To truly thrive in your role as a church leader, it is essential to seek out both accountability and mentorship. These two pillars of support can help strengthen your foundations in faith and ensure that you are equipped to oversee the challenges that come with leading a congregation. By seeking out individuals who can hold you accountable and provide guidance and wisdom, you will be better prepared to navigate the difficulties of ministry.

Accountability is crucial for church leaders, as it helps to keep us grounded and focused on our mission. By having someone to answer to, we are more likely to stay true to our values and commitments. Whether it be a fellow pastor, a trusted friend, or a mentor, having someone who can hold us to a higher standard can help us grow in our faith and leadership abilities.

Accountability also provides a sense of community and support, reminding us that we are not alone in our journey.

Mentorship is equally important for church leaders, as it allows us to learn from those who have walked the path before us. A mentor can provide valuable insights, wisdom, and guidance that can help us navigate the challenges of ministry with grace and resilience. By seeking out a mentor who has experience in church leadership, we can learn from their successes and failures, gaining valuable knowledge that can help us avoid common pitfalls and grow in our faith.

When seeking out accountability and mentorship, it is important to be intentional and proactive. Reach out to individuals who you admire and respect and ask them to come alongside you on your journey. Be open to feedback and willing to learn from those who have more experience than you. Remember that seeking out accountability and mentorship is not a sign of weakness, but rather a sign of strength and a desire to grow and improve as a leader.

Seeking accountability and mentorship is essential for church leaders who want to strengthen their foundations in faith and build resilience in their ministry. By surrounding yourself with individuals who can hold you accountable and provide guidance and wisdom, you will be better equipped to manage the challenges that come with leading a congregation. Remember that you are not alone in your journey and that there are individuals who are willing to come alongside you and support you in your role as a church leader.

Staying Grounded in Prayer and Scripture

As church leaders and members of Christian organizations, it is essential to stay grounded in prayer and scripture to build and maintain spiritual resilience. In times of uncertainty and challenges, turning to God through prayer and seeking guidance from His word can provide the strength and comfort needed to navigate through demanding situations. By prioritizing prayer and scripture in our daily lives, we can strengthen our foundations in faith and be better equipped to lead and serve others effectively.

> Prayer is a powerful tool that allows us to communicate with God and seek His guidance, wisdom, and strength. It is through prayer that we can express our deepest concerns, fears, and hopes to God, knowing that He hears and answers our prayers according to His will. By making prayer a priority in our lives, we can experience a deeper connection with God and draw closer to Him in times of need. As church leaders, it is important to model a lifestyle of prayer and encourage others to do the same, creating a community that is grounded in faith and reliant on God's guidance.

Scripture serves as a source of wisdom, comfort, and encouragement for Christians. The Bible is filled with promises and truths that can sustain us through trials and tribulations. By regularly reading and meditating on scripture, we can cultivate a deeper understanding of God's character and His plans for us. As church leaders, it is crucial to prioritize the study of scripture and to share its teachings with others, helping them to grow in their faith and resilience. By grounding ourselves in the truth of God's word, we can find hope and strength to persevere in the face of adversity.

Incorporating prayer and scripture into our daily routines can help us stay grounded in our faith and maintain a durable foundation in Christ. By setting aside time each day for prayer and reading the Bible, we can nurture our relationship with God and deepen our understanding of His will for our lives. As church leaders, it is important to lead by example and demonstrate the importance of prayer and scripture in building spiritual resilience. By encouraging others to prioritize prayer and scripture in their lives, we can create a community that is rooted in faith and equipped to face any challenge that comes their way.

Staying grounded in prayer and living in an active prayer life and scripture is essential for building and maintaining spiritual resilience as church leaders and members of Christian organizations. By making prayer a priority and regularly studying scripture, we can deepen our relationship with God and draw strength from His word. As we cultivate a lifestyle of prayer and scripture reading, we can build a solid foundation in faith that will sustain us through trials and empower us to lead and serve others effectively. Let us commit to staying grounded in prayer and scripture, trusting in God's faithfulness, and seeking His guidance in all that we do.

Embracing Change and Adaptability

Change is an inevitable part of life, and as church leaders, it is crucial that we embrace change with open arms and a cheerful outlook. To thrive in today's ever-evolving world, we must cultivate a spirit of adaptability and flexibility within our churches and organizations. Embracing change allows us to grow and evolve, leading us to new opportunities for spiritual growth and outreach.

As we navigate the challenges and uncertainties of the modern world, it is essential that we remain rooted in our faith and trust in God's plan for us. By embracing change and adapting to new circumstances, we demonstrate our resilience and commitment to serving our communities with grace and compassion. Remember, change is not something to be feared, but rather a chance for us to strengthen our foundations in faith and grow closer to God.

In times of transition and uncertainty, it is important for church leaders to lead by example and show our congregations the power of resilience and adaptability. By remaining steadfast in our faith and demonstrating a willingness to embrace change, we inspire those around us to do the same. Our ability to adapt to new challenges and circumstances is a testament to the strength of our foundations in faith and the power of God's love in our lives.

As we continue to navigate the ever-changing landscape of the modern world, let us remember that change is not a hindrance, but an opportunity for growth and renewal. By embracing change and adapting to new circumstances, we demonstrate our commitment to serving God and our communities with love and compassion. Let us remain steadfast in our faith, trusting in God's plan for us and allowing His guidance to lead us through any challenges that may come our way.

For church leaders, it is our responsibility to embrace change and adaptability with open hearts and minds. By cultivating a spirit of resilience and flexibility within our organizations, we can weather any storm and emerge stronger than ever. Let us continue to strengthen our foundations in faith and trust in God's plan for us, knowing that He will guide us through any challenges that may come our way. Embrace change, adapt with grace, and watch as God's blessings unfold in our churches, organizations, and communities.

Trusting God's Guidance in Decision-Making

Trusting God's guidance in decision-making is a fundamental aspect of Christian resilience. As church leaders, it is crucial to rely on God's wisdom and direction when faced with difficult choices. By seeking God's guidance through prayer, meditation, and reflection on scripture, we can be confident that we are making decisions that align with His will for our lives and ministries.

In times of uncertainty and doubt, it can be tempting to rely on our understanding or the advice of others. However, as Christians, we are called to trust in the Lord with all our hearts and lean not on our understanding (Proverbs 3:5). By surrendering our decisions to God and seeking His guidance, we can have peace knowing that He will direct our paths in the way that is best for us.

Churches and non-profit organizations can benefit from trusting in God's guidance in decision-making. By seeking His wisdom and direction, we can ensure that our ministries are aligned with His purposes and are successful in furthering His kingdom. When we trust in God's guidance, we can have confidence that He will provide the resources, opportunities, and support needed to accomplish His will.

Trusting in God's guidance also helps to build spiritual resilience within church leadership. When we rely on God's wisdom rather than our own, we are better equipped to manage challenges, setbacks, and obstacles that may come our way. By trusting in God's guidance, we can cultivate a spirit of perseverance, faith, and hope that will enable us to overcome any adversity that we may face.

Placing your trust in God's guidance in decision-making is essential for building Christian resilience within church leadership and organizations.

By seeking His wisdom, direction, and will, we can be confident that we are making decisions that align with His purposes and will lead to success in our ministries. Let us continue to trust in God's guidance, knowing that He will never lead us astray and will always provide for us in every situation.

Inspiring Others Through Your Resilience

In times of uncertainty and challenge, it is essential for church leaders to demonstrate resilience and strength in their faith. By embodying a spirit of perseverance and determination, you have the power to inspire others through your actions and words. Your resilience in the face of adversity can serve as a beacon of hope for those who are struggling to find their way in the darkness.

When you show resilience in your faith, you are showing others that it is possible to overcome even the most difficult of circumstances. Your unwavering commitment to your beliefs can serve as a source of strength for those who are feeling lost or hopeless. By sharing your own struggles and victories, you can show others that they are not alone in their journey and that there is always a light at the end of the tunnel.

As church leaders, it is important to remember that your actions speak louder than words. By demonstrating resilience in your faith, you are setting an example for others to follow. Your ability to weather the storms of life with grace and dignity can inspire those around you to do the same. By showing others that it is possible to find peace and strength amid chaos, you are helping to build a community of believers united in their faith.

In times of doubt and fear, losing sight of the bigger picture is easy. However, by embodying resilience in your faith, you can help others to see that there is always a greater purpose at work. Your ability to stay grounded in your beliefs, even when faced with adversity, can remind others that God is always present and guiding us through our struggles. By sharing your own experiences of resilience, you can help others to find hope and courage in their journey.

By demonstrating resilience in your faith, you are strengthening your foundation and building a solid and resilient community of believers. Your ability to inspire others through your actions and words can help to create a culture of resilience within your church and beyond. By showing others that it is possible to weather the storms of life with grace and courage, you are helping build a community grounded in faith and united in purpose. Remember, your resilience can inspire others to find strength and hope in their journey of faith.

Equipping Church Leaders with Resilience Tools

In today's fast-paced and constantly changing world, church leaders face numerous challenges that can assess their faith and resilience. It is crucial for church leaders to be equipped with the necessary tools and strategies to navigate through these challenges with grace and strength. This subchapter, "Equipping Church Leaders with Resilience Tools," aims to provide practical advice and guidance for church leaders on how to strengthen their foundations in faith and build resilience in the face of adversity.

> One of the key resilience tools for church leaders is prayer and meditation. By spending time in prayer and connecting with God on a regular basis, church leaders can find comfort, guidance, and strength to face whatever challenges come their way. Prayer can also help church leaders to maintain a positive mindset and trust in God's plan, even when things seem difficult or overwhelming.

Another important resilience tool for church leaders is community and support. Building a solid network of fellow church leaders, mentors, and friends can provide invaluable encouragement and accountability. By surrounding themselves with a supportive community, church leaders can share their struggles, seek advice, and receive prayer and encouragement when needed. This sense of belonging and connectedness can help church leaders to stay resilient and grounded in their faith.

Church leaders can also benefit from developing healthy habits and self-care routines. Taking care of their physical, emotional, and mental well-being is essential for maintaining resilience and strength. This can include setting boundaries, practicing mindfulness, getting regular exercise, eating well, and getting enough rest. By prioritizing self-care, church leaders can recharge and refuel, allowing them to serve their communities better and fulfill their calling with joy and passion.

Lastly, church leaders can strengthen their resilience by staying rooted in their faith and the Word of God. By studying scripture, attending worship services, and participating in spiritual practices, church leaders can deepen their relationship with God and draw strength from His promises and truth. This foundation in faith can provide a solid anchor in times of trouble and uncertainty, helping church leaders to stay resilient and steadfast in their calling. By equipping church leaders with these resilience tools, we can empower them to navigate the challenges of ministry with grace, courage, and unwavering faith.

Providing Resources for Personal Growth and Development

To foster Christian resilience within our church communities, it is essential to provide resources for personal growth and development. By offering opportunities for individuals to deepen their faith, strengthen their spiritual foundations, and cultivate a sense of purpose and meaning, we can empower them to navigate life's challenges with grace and strength. As church leaders and foundations, it is our responsibility to support and encourage the growth of those within our congregations, equipping them with the tools they need to thrive in their spiritual journey.

One way to provide resources for personal growth and development is through educational programs and workshops. These programs offer a wealth of knowledge and practical tools for individuals to deepen their theological understanding, spiritual formation, and personal reflection. By engaging in these opportunities, individuals can strengthen their relationship with God and gain resilience in navigating life's challenges, such as stress, grief, or conflict.

In addition to educational programs, it is essential to offer resources for personal growth and development through spiritual practices and disciplines. These practices, such as regular prayer, meditation, scripture reading, and worship, bring a sense of peace, clarity, and purpose, helping individuals to navigate life's challenges with faith and resilience.

Furthermore, providing resources for personal growth and development can also involve creating opportunities for individuals to serve others and engage in acts of compassion and justice. By encouraging individuals to volunteer, participate in mission trips, or support local non-profit organizations, we can help them develop a sense of empathy, compassion, and social responsibility. These experiences can not only deepen their faith and strengthen their spiritual resilience but also help them to make a positive impact in their communities and the world.

By providing resources for personal growth and development, we can empower individuals within our church communities to deepen their faith, strengthen their spiritual foundations, and cultivate resilience in the face of life's challenges. As church leaders, foundations, and non-profit organizations, it is our duty to support and encourage the growth of those within our congregations, equipping them with the They need the tools to thrive in their spiritual journey. Together, we can create a community of individuals who are strong in their faith, resilient in their spirits, and committed to living out their beliefs in the world.

Encouraging a Resilient Mindset in Non-Profit Organizations

Resilience is a critical factor in achieving success and making a lasting impact on the community in the world of non-profit organizations. As church leaders and members of foundations, we must foster a resilient mindset within our organizations. This mindset involves overcoming challenges and continuing to serve those in need, drawing strength from our faith and inspiring others to do the same.

One powerful way to foster a resilient mindset in non-profit organizations is by underlining the significance of spiritual resilience. As Christians, we passionately believe that our faith equips us with the strength and courage to confront adversity. By turning to God in times of trouble and seeking guidance through prayer and scripture, we can construct a sturdy foundation of resilience that will carry us through the toughest of times, instilling hope, and trust in our hearts.

Another way to promote resilience within our organizations is by creating a supportive and nurturing environment for our members. By offering encouragement, understanding, and compassion to struggling people, we can help them develop the resilience they need to overcome obstacles and continue their essential work. We can create a space where individuals feel empowered to persevere in adversity by fostering a sense of community and belonging.

Leading by example is not plainly important, it is crucial when it comes to resilience. As church leaders and members of foundations, we must not only demonstrate resilience in our own lives, but also show others how to overcome challenges with grace and strength. By sharing our personal stories of resilience and highlighting the ways in which our faith has guided us through tough times, we can inspire others to develop their own resilient mindset and trust in God's plan for their lives. Let us inspire and motivate each other.

Enchanting a resilient mindset in non-profit organizations is essential for building a solid foundation of faith and service. By emphasizing spiritual resilience, creating a supportive environment, and leading by example, we can inspire others to develop the strength they need to overcome challenges and continue their essential work in the community. Let us work together to strengthen our foundations in faith and build a culture of resilience that will sustain us through any storm.

> Learning how to embrace resilience as a foundation in faith is essential for church leaders to navigate the challenges and obstacles that may come their way. The journey of leadership within the church is not always easy. Still, by leaning on the strength of our faith and cultivating a mindset of resilience, we can persevere and continue to lead with grace and humility. Church leaders play a crucial role in guiding and shepherding their congregations, and they must equip themselves with the tools necessary to weather the storms that may arise. By embracing resilience, leaders can model for their communities how to face adversity with courage and hope, trusting in God's steadfast love and faithfulness.

As we reflect on the importance of resilience in our faith journey, let us remember that we are not alone in our struggles. God is with us every step of the way, providing us with the strength and endurance we need to press on. By anchoring ourselves in our faith and leaning on the support of our communities, we can find the fortitude to overcome any obstacles that come our way. Church leaders must prioritize self-care and spiritual nourishment to cultivate resilience as a foundation in faith. This means resting, recharging, and reconnecting with God through prayer, meditation, and scripture. Leaders can better serve their congregations by prioritizing their well-being and leading with wisdom and compassion.

Let us embrace resilience as a foundation in our faith journey, trusting in God's provision and guidance. By cultivating a spirit of resilience, church leaders can navigate leadership challenges with grace and strength, inspiring their communities to do the same. May we continue to lean on our faith as we face the uncertainties of life, knowing that God is faithful and will sustain us through it all.

LESSON
6

I Have Failed

Maintaining a Positive Mindset

Let's face it, we all have that pesky little voice in our heads that loves to point out our flaws and shortcomings. But it's time to show that inner critic who's boss! Take a moment to reflect on all the things you've accomplished in your life – big or small. From mastering the art of parallel parking to landing that dream job, you've done some impressive stuff. Admit to yourself you have done something or something no one has done before, has yet to still do, or is struggling to do. Celebrate yourself for a change.

> "Value your dreams by believing that they are already coming true."
>
> - ETHAN R. ESBACH

Strategies for Preventing Negative Self-Talk Relapses

So, you've been working hard to silence that pesky inner critic of yours, huh? Good for you! But let's face it, old habits die hard, and negative self-talk has a way of sneaking back in when we least expect it. Don't worry, though - I've got some strategies to help you prevent those relapses and keep that inner critic quiet once and for all.

First things first, you've got to stay vigilant. Like a ninja on a mission, you need to be on the lookout for any signs of negative self-talk trying to creep back in. Pay attention to those sneaky little thoughts that start with "I can't" or "I'm not good enough" and shut them down before they take hold.

Next, surround yourself with positivity. Fill your life with people who lift you up and encourage you to be your best self. Avoid those Negative Nellies who only bring you down and make you doubt yourself. Remember, you are the company you keep, so choose wisely. Another strategy for preventing negative self-talk relapses is to practice self-care. Take time for yourself to do things that make you feel good, whether it's taking a bubble bath, going for a walk in nature, or indulging in your favourite guilty pleasure. When you take care of yourself, you're less likely to fall back into old patterns of negative thinking.

And don't forget to challenge those negative thoughts when they do pop up. Ask yourself if there's any evidence to support them, or if they're just your inner critic trying to bring you down. Remember, you have the power to change your thoughts and beliefs, so don't let that pesky inner critic win. Finally, be kind to yourself. We all have bad days and moments of self-doubt, but that doesn't mean you're a failure. Cut yourself some slack, practice self-compassion, and remember that you are worthy of love and respect, no matter what that inner critic might try to tell you. With these strategies in your back pocket, you'll be well-equipped to prevent those negative self-talk relapses and keep that inner critic at bay. You've got this!

Self-Care Practices for Nurturing a Healthy Mindset

Are you tired of that little voice in your head always telling you that you're not good enough? Well, it's time to shut that inner critic up once and for all! In this subchapter, we'll explore some self-care practices that will help you nurture a healthy mindset and silence that negative self-talk for good.

First up, we have the classic self-care practice of pampering yourself. Treat yourself to a relaxing bath, a massage, or a spa day. Take some time to unwind and show yourself some love. After all, you deserve it! And who knows, maybe your inner critic will take a back seat while you're busy being fabulous.

Next, let's talk about the importance of exercise for maintaining a healthy mindset. Exercise not only improves physical health, but it also releases endorphins, those feel-good chemicals that can help combat negative self-talk. So go for a run, take a yoga class, or dance like nobody's watching.

Your mind will thank you for it! Another self-care practice to consider is journaling. Writing down your thoughts and feelings can be a powerful tool for processing emotions and gaining perspective on your inner dialogue. Plus, it's a great way to track your progress as you work towards silencing that inner critic. So, grab a pen and paper and start journaling your way to a healthier mindset.

In addition to these practices, don't forget the power of positive affirmations. Repeat phrases like "I am enough," "I am worthy," and "I am capable" to yourself daily. Over time, these affirmations can help rewire your brain to focus on the positive rather than the negative. So go ahead, give yourself a pep talk and watch your mindset shift for the better.

And finally, remember to surround yourself with positive influences. Whether it's friends, family, or mentors, having a support system can make all the difference in overcoming self-limiting beliefs and negative self-talk. So don't be afraid to lean on those who lift you up and encourage you to be your best self. With these self-care practices in your arsenal, you'll be well on your way to silencing that inner critic and nurturing a healthy mindset that empowers you to thrive.

Finding Joy and Gratitude in Everyday Moments

Are you tired of constantly criticizing yourself and feeling like you're never good enough? It's time to silence that inner critic and start finding joy and gratitude in everyday moments. Yes, even those moments when you accidentally spill your coffee all over your desk or when you trip over your own feet in front of your crush. Embrace the humour in those situations and laugh at yourself instead of berating yourself.

One way to find joy and gratitude in everyday moments is to practice mindfulness. Take a moment to appreciate the little things around you, like the smell of freshly cut grass or the sound of birds chirping in the morning. It's amazing how much beauty there is in the world when we take the time to notice it. And hey, even if you step in a puddle on your way to work, at least you can appreciate the refreshing coolness on a hot day.

Another way to combat negative self-talk and find joy in everyday moments is to surround yourself with positive people. Spend time with friends who lift you up and make you laugh. Laughter truly is the best medicine, and it's hard to feel down on yourself when you're laughing until your stomach hurts. Plus, having a support system of people who believe in you can help drown out that pesky inner critic.

Remember, it's okay to make mistakes and have off days. Nobody is perfect, and that's what makes us human. Instead of beating yourself up over every little blunder, try to find the humour in it. Did you accidentally send a text to the wrong person? Maybe it will turn into a funny story you can laugh about later. Embrace your imperfections and learn to love yourself flaws and all.

So, the next time you find yourself being overly critical of yourself, take a step back and try to find joy and gratitude in the moment. Life is too short to be constantly tearing yourself down. Embrace the humour in everyday mishaps and surround yourself with positivity. You'll be amazed at how much happier and more confident you feel when you silence that inner critic and focus on the good things in life.

Embracing Your Inner Cheerleader - Acknowledging Your Strengths and Accomplishments

Acknowledging Your Strengths and Accomplishments explores the importance of recognizing and celebrating your unique abilities and successes. So, sit back, relax, and get ready to give yourself a well-deserved pat on the back figuratively, of course

Let's face it, we all have that pesky little voice in our heads that loves to point out our flaws and shortcomings. But it's time to show that inner critic who's boss! Take a moment to reflect on all the things you've accomplished in your life – big or small. From mastering the art of parallel parking to landing that dream job, you've done some impressive stuff. Admit to yourself you have done something or something no one has done before, has yet to still do, or is struggling to do. Celebrate yourself for a change.

Now, I know what you're thinking – "But I'm not perfect, I still have so much to work on." Well, guess what? Nobody is perfect! Embrace your imperfections and quirks, they're what make you unique. Remember, it is okay to be a work in progress. If you're trying to grow and improve, that's what truly matters.

So, take a break from the self-criticism and start giving yourself a little credit where credit is due. Maybe you're a fantastic cook, a great listener, or a master multitasker. Whatever your strengths may be, own them! Celebrate your victories, no matter how small they may seem. You deserve to feel proud of yourself. Acknowledging your strengths and accomplishments is an essential step in silencing that inner critic once and for all. So go ahead, give yourself a high five (metaphorically, of course), and keep on shining bright. Remember, you can achieve great things – all it takes is a little self-love and belief in yourself.

Cultivating a Supportive Inner Dialogue

Are you tired of that little voice in your head constantly criticizing everything you do? Well, it's time to shut that inner critic up and start cultivating a more supportive inner dialogue! In this subchapter, we'll explore some humorous and effective ways to tackle negative self-talk and overcome self-limiting beliefs once and for all.

First things first, let's acknowledge that we all have that pesky inner critic who loves to rain on our parade. But guess what? You don't have to listen to it! Instead, try giving that voice a silly name like "Debbie Downer" or "Negative Nancy" to take away its power. Trust me, it's hard to take criticism seriously when it's coming from someone named Debbie.

Next, it's time to reframe those negative thoughts into something more positive and supportive. For example, instead of thinking, "I can't do this," try saying, "I may not be able to do it yet, but I'm working on it." See what we did there? By adding a little humour and self-compassion, you can start to shift your mindset and believe in your abilities.

Another fun exercise to cultivate a supportive inner dialogue is to imagine that your inner critic is a hilarious stand-up comedian. Picture them telling you all the ridiculous things that make you doubt yourself, but in a way that's so over-the-top and absurd that you can't help but laugh. Suddenly, those negative thoughts don't seem so powerful anymore, do they?

Don't forget to surround yourself with positive influences and supportive people who lift you up instead of tearing you down. Remember, you are the company you keep, so choose wisely. And hey, if all else fails, just blast your favourite cheesy '80s power ballad and dance around your living room like nobody's watching. Sometimes a little laughter and music are all you need to drown out that inner critic once and for all.

Cultivating a supportive inner dialogue doesn't have to be a daunting task. With a little humour, self-compassion, and a willingness to challenge those negative beliefs, you can start to silence that inner critic and embrace a more positive mindset. So go ahead, give yourself a pat on the back, crack a joke at your own expense, and watch as your self-limiting beliefs crumble before your eyes. You've got this!

Sharing Your Journey of Overcoming Negative Self-Talk

Are you tired of constantly hearing that annoying voice in your head telling you that you're not good enough? Well, you're not alone! We've all been there, battling with our inner critic and their never-ending stream of negative self-talk. But fear not, my fellow adults, for there is hope! In this subchapter, we will discuss the importance of sharing your journey of overcoming negative self-talk with others.

First and foremost, sharing your journey of overcoming negative self-talk can be incredibly empowering. By opening to others about your struggles, you not only validate your own experiences but also show others that they are not alone in their own battles. It's like forming a support group for your inner critic – except this time, you're the one in charge!

Secondly, sharing your journey can help you gain valuable insights and perspectives from others. Sometimes we are so stuck in our own negative thought patterns that we can't see the forest for the trees. By talking to others about your struggles, you may discover new strategies and techniques for silencing your inner critic that you never would have thought of on your own. Plus, it's always nice to have a good laugh at the ridiculous things our inner critic comes up with, am I right?

Furthermore, sharing your journey can inspire others to act and start their own journey of overcoming negative self-talk. Your story has the power to motivate and encourage others to confront their inner critic head-on and challenge their self-limiting beliefs. Who knows, you might just become the beacon of hope for someone who thought they were stuck in a never-ending cycle of negative self-talk.

Sharing your journey of overcoming negative self-talk is not only beneficial for yourself but also for those around you. So go ahead, be brave, and start talking about your experiences. Remember, we're all in this together, fighting against our inner critics one ridiculous thought at a time. And hey, who knows, maybe one day we'll all look back and laugh at how silly we were to let our inner critic control us for so long. It's time to take back control and silence that pesky voice once and for all!

Reflecting on Your Growth and Progress

As you continue your journey of silencing your inner critic and overcoming negative self-talk, it's important to take a moment to reflect on your growth and progress. After all, you've come a long way from that voice in your head telling you that you're not good enough or that you'll never succeed. So, grab a mirror, give yourself a high five, and let's celebrate how far you've come!

> Remember when you used to believe every negative thought that popped into your head? Like when you thought you couldn't possibly finish that project on time or that you were destined to fail at every new endeavour. Well, look at you now, proving that inner critic wrong time and time again! You've learned to challenge those self-limiting beliefs and replace them with positive affirmations. Who knew you had it in you to be your own cheerleader?

Think about all the times you've faced challenges head-on and come out stronger on the other side. Whether it was overcoming a fear, stepping out of your comfort zone, or simply showing yourself some much-needed self-love, you've shown incredible growth and resilience. And let's not forget the progress you've made in recognizing and shutting down that negative self-talk. It's like you've built a fortress around your mind, protecting yourself from those pesky little critics.

So, take a moment to pat yourself on the back (figuratively, of course) and bask in the glow of your own awesomeness. You've worked hard to get to this point, and you deserve to celebrate your victories, no matter how big or small. Remember, progress is not always linear, and setbacks are just opportunities for growth. So, keep pushing forward, keep challenging those self-limiting beliefs, and keep silencing that inner critic like the boss you are!

In the wise words of an unknown philosopher (probably someone on Twitter), "Don't forget to be proud of yourself and how far you've come. You're doing a great job, sweetie!" So go forth, my fellow self-talk warriors, and continue your path to self-acceptance, self-love, and a whole lot of laughter along the way. Because hey, if you can't laugh at yourself, who can you laugh at?

Embracing Your Authentic Self

Are you tired of constantly feeling like you're not good enough? Do you find yourself listening to that pesky inner critic on repeat, telling you that you're not smart enough, not pretty enough, not successful enough? Well, it's time to shut that little voice up and start embracing your authentic self!

Let's face it, we all have our flaws and quirks that make us unique. Instead of trying to fit into society's mold of perfection, why not embrace the things that make you, well, you? Maybe you have a weird sense of humour or a love for cheesy 80s music - whatever it is, own it!

One of the first steps to embracing your authentic self is to silence that inner critic once and for all. Every time it starts chirping away with negative self-talk, tell it to take a hike! You are amazing just the way you are, flaws and all. Remember, perfection is boring - it's your imperfections that make you interesting.

Another important aspect of embracing your authentic self is learning to love and accept yourself unconditionally. Stop comparing yourself to others and start appreciating the unique qualities that make you who you are. Whether you're a little quirky, a bit awkward, or just downright weird, those are the things that make you special.

So, let go of the need for approval from others and start living life on your own terms. Embrace your authentic self and watch as your confidence soars and your inner critic fades into the background. Remember, you are enough, just as you are. So go ahead, be yourself—the world will thank you for it!

Moving Forward with Confidence and Self-Love

Congratulations, my fellow adults! You have made it this far in the journey of self-discovery and self-improvement. Now, it's time to kick that pesky inner critic to the curb and move forward with confidence and self-love. Trust me, you deserve it!

First things first, let's address that inner critic of yours. You know, the one that loves to tell you that you're not good enough, smart enough, or capable enough. Well, guess what? That voice is about as helpful as a screen door on a submarine. So, let's silence it once and for all with a healthy dose of humour and self-love.

Now, repeat after me: "I am fabulous, fierce, and unstoppable!" Say it loud and proud, my friends. Believe in yourself and all that you are capable of. Remember, you are the master of your own destiny, and no negative self-talk can stand in your way when you have confidence and self-love on your side.

It's time to embrace your uniqueness and celebrate your quirks. Who cares if you snort when you laugh or have a weird obsession with collecting rubber ducks? Own it, my friends! Embrace your individuality and let your freak flag fly high. After all, life is too short to be anything but your wonderfully weird self.

So, as you continue this journey of overcoming self-limiting beliefs and negative self-talk, remember to laugh at yourself, love yourself, and keep moving forward with confidence. You have got this, my fellow adults. And remember, the only voice that truly matters is the one within you who believes in your own awesomeness. So go forth and conquer, with a smile on your face and a heart full of self-love.

LESSON 7

Fair and Square

Unmasking the Inner Critic

Setting goals and acting are crucial steps in silencing that pesky inner critic that loves to rain on your parade. But hey, don't worry, we've got your back! In this subchapter, we'll dive into how to set achievable goals and follow through on them, all while keeping that negative self-talk at bay.

> "It's better to have one focused goal than to have many goals and worry about them."
>
> – ETHAN R. ESBACH

Are you tired of that little voice in your head constantly criticizing your every move? Well, it's time to unmask the inner critic and show it who's boss! I'll explore the sneaky ways our inner critic tries to hold us back and learn how to silence it once and for all.

Picture this: you're about to try something new and exciting, but just as you're getting ready to take the leap, your inner critic chimes in with a laundry list of reasons why you shouldn't bother. It's like having a tiny heckler living rent-free in your brain! Here are some tools to combat this pesky little voice and reclaim our confidence. One of the first steps in unmasking the inner critic is to recognize when it's speaking up.

Pay attention to the negative self-talk that pops into your mind when you're faced with a challenge or opportunity. Is it telling you that you're not good enough, smart enough, or worthy enough to succeed? Once you start to identify these patterns, you can begin to challenge and reframe them with more positive and empowering thoughts.

Another key strategy for silencing the inner critic is to practice self-compassion. Instead of beating yourself up for making mistakes or falling short of your own expectations, try treating yourself with the same kindness and understanding you would offer a friend in a similar situation. Remember, nobody's perfect, and it's okay to cut yourself some slack now and then.

So, the next time your inner critic starts to rear its ugly head, don't be afraid to give it a piece of your mind. Show it that you're in charge and that its negative chatter is no match for your self-confidence and determination. With a little humour and a lot of self-love, you can finally silence that pesky inner critic and step into your full potential. So go ahead, take that leap, and watch as your inner critic fades into the background where it belongs!

The Origin Story of Your Inner Critic

Have you ever stopped to wonder where that pesky little voice in your head comes from? You know, the one that always seems to have something negative to say about everything you do? Well, let me tell you a little story about the origin of your inner critic. Once upon a time, in a far-off land called Childhood, there lived a little creature known as the Inner Critic. This critter was born out of a combination of societal expectations, past experiences, and a touch of good old-fashioned self-doubt. From the moment you took your first steps, the Inner Critic was there, ready to whisper in your ear about all the ways you could have done better. As you grew older, the Inner Critic grew stronger, feeding off your insecurities and fears. It learned to mimic the voices of authority figures in your life, like parents, teachers, and even that mean girl from fifth grade who said your hair looked weird.

Before you knew it, the Inner Critic had taken up residence in your mind, constantly chattering away about your shortcomings and failures. But here's the thing – the Inner Critic isn't all bad. In fact, it's just trying to protect you from getting hurt. It's like that overprotective parent who won't let you ride your bike without a helmet, even though you're a grown adult. The Inner Critic means well, it's just a little... misguided.

The next time you hear that familiar voice in your head telling you that you're not good enough, take a moment to thank your Inner Critic for trying to keep you safe. And then kindly remind it that you're a capable, competent adult who can handle whatever life throws your way. After all, who needs a nagging little creature in their head when they've got all the tools, they need to silence it once and for all?

The Inner Critic's Greatest Hits

Have you ever noticed that your inner critic seems to have a playlist of its greatest hits on repeat? It's like a never-ending loop of negative self-talk that plays in your mind, telling you all the reasons why you're not good enough. But fear not, dear reader, for in this chapter we will be dissecting some of the Inner Critic's greatest hits and learning how to silence them once and for all.

> First up on the Inner Critic's Greatest Hits album is the classic track "You're not smart enough." This hit single likes to pop up whenever you're faced with a challenging task or trying to learn something new. But let me tell you, dear reader, intelligence comes in many forms, and just because you may struggle with one thing doesn't mean you're not smart. So next time this tune starts playing, hit pause and remind yourself of all the things you do know.
>
> Next on the playlist is the timeless ballad "You're not good enough." This track loves to rear its ugly head whenever you're feeling insecure or comparing yourself to others. But remember, dear reader, you are

unique and worthy just as you are. So, when this song starts playing, crank up the volume on self-love and dance to your own beat.

Then we have the upbeat tune "You'll never succeed." This catchy track likes to play whenever you're stepping out of your comfort zone or pursuing your dreams. But don't let this song dampen your spirit, dear reader. Success looks different for everyone, and the only way to fail is to never try. So, turn up the volume on your determination and prove that Inner Critic wrong.

The Inner Critic's Greatest Hits album wouldn't be complete without the power ballad "You're too old to change." This song loves to play when you're considering making positive changes in your life or stepping outside of your routine. But age is just a number, dear reader, and it's never too late to learn, grow, and evolve.

When this track starts playing, hit repeat on the belief that change is always possible. And finally, we have the classic anthem "You're not worthy of love." This heartbreaking tune likes to play when you're feeling lonely or struggling with self-acceptance. But remember, dear reader, you are deserving of love and belonging just as you are. So, when this song starts playing, sing along to the melody of self-compassion and remind yourself that you are enough.

The Inner Critic's Greatest Hits may be catchy, but they are not the truth. It's time to change the tune and silence that negative self-talk once and for all. So, grab your headphones, turn up the volume on self-love, and dance to the beat of your own worthiness. You've got this!

Thriving Beyond Self-Limiting Beliefs - Setting Goals and Acting

Setting goals and acting are crucial steps in silencing that pesky inner critic that loves to rain on your parade. But hey, don't worry, we've got your back! In this subchapter, we'll dive into how to set achievable goals and follow through on them, all while keeping that negative self-talk at bay.

First things first, let's talk about setting goals. Now, I know what you're thinking - setting goals can seem daunting and overwhelming. But fear not, my friend! Start by breaking down your big goals into smaller, more manageable tasks. Think of it as eating a giant pizza - you wouldn't try to shove the whole thing in your mouth at once, right? (Well, maybe you would, but that's a whole other issue we'll address later).

Once you've got your goals set, it's time to act! This is where the rubber meets the road, so to speak. Decide, create a timeline, and get moving. Remember, progress is progress, no matter how small. So even if you only manage to take one tiny step towards your goal, pat yourself on the back and celebrate like you just won the lottery (okay, maybe not that extreme, but you get the idea).

Now, we know that pesky inner critic of yours is probably whispering sweet nothings in your ear, trying to derail your progress. But don't let that negative self-talk get the best of you! Challenge those thoughts with positive affirmations and reminders of your past successes. And hey, if all else fails, you can always picture your inner critic as a grumpy old man yelling at a cloud.

Trust me, it works like a charm. So, there you have it, folks - setting goals and acting doesn't have to be a daunting task. With a little humour, a positive attitude, and a whole lot of determination, you can kick that inner critic to the curb and achieve your wildest dreams. So go forth, my friends, and conquer those goals like the badass warriors you are!

Surrounding Yourself with Positive Influences

Are you tired of that little voice in your head constantly telling you that you're not good enough? Well, it's time to shut that inner critic up once and for all! In this subchapter, we will explore the importance of surrounding yourself with positive influences to help combat those negative thoughts.

First and foremost, it's essential to surround yourself with people who uplift and support you. Surround yourself with friends who believe in you and encourage you to chase your dreams. Remember, you are the company you keep, so choose wisely! And if you find yourself surrounded by negative Nancys, it may be time to reevaluate your social circle.

In addition to surrounding yourself with positive people, it's crucial to consume positive content. Whether it's reading motivational books, listening to inspiring podcasts, or watching uplifting movies, fill your mind with positivity. Trust me, it's much better than binge-watching a depressing drama that leaves you feeling like a hot mess.

Another way to surround yourself with positive influences is to practice gratitude daily. Take a few minutes each day to reflect on what you're grateful for. It could be something as simple as a delicious cup of coffee or a warm hug from a loved one. Gratitude can shift your perspective from focusing on what's wrong to appreciating what's right in your life.

And finally, don't forget to be your own cheerleader! Celebrate your wins, no matter how small they may seem. Give yourself a pat on the back for that presentation at work or for finally conquering that yoga pose. Remember, you are your biggest supporter, so don't be afraid to give yourself some love and encouragement. Surrounding yourself with positive influences starts with you, so let's silence that inner critic and start living our best lives!

Celebrating Your Progress and Successes

Are you ready to throw a party for yourself? That's right, it's time to celebrate your progress and successes in overcoming those pesky self-limiting beliefs and negative self-talk! Grab your party hat (or crown, if you're feeling fancy) and get ready to toast to all the hard work you've put in to silence that inner critic once and for all.

> Now, I know what you're thinking - celebrating yourself? Isn't that a little egotistical? Well, let me tell you, there's nothing wrong with patting yourself on the back every now and then. In fact, it's essential to acknowledge and celebrate your wins, big or small. So go ahead, give yourself a high five or a fist bump - you deserve it!

As you reflect on your journey to overcoming self-limiting beliefs and negative self-talk, take a moment to appreciate how far you've come. Remember that time you doubted yourself but pushed through anyway? Or when you silenced that inner critic and took a leap of faith? Those are the moments worth celebrating - because they show just how resilient and capable you truly are.

How should you celebrate your progress and successes? Well, the options are endless! Treat yourself to a spa day, indulge in your favourite meal, or take a moment to bask in your accomplishments. And don't forget to share your wins with friends and family - they'll be happy to cheer you on and celebrate with you.

> Celebrating your progress and successes is not about being boastful or arrogant. It's about recognizing your worth, acknowledging your growth, and embracing the journey of self-improvement. So go ahead, throw yourself a party, dance like nobody is watching, and revel in the joy of knowing that you are on your way to silencing that inner critic for good! Cheers to you, my friend!

I truly hope the lessons and principles discussed not only allow you to meet your new self or discover new and innovative ways to build a resilient you but also that these lessons remain with you and that this book becomes your reference guide in the future.

Be Resilient!

REFERENCES

1. Exploring the Historic Trends of Crypto Market Cycles: Lessons Learned | Fingerlakes1.com. https://www.fingerlakes1.com/2023/04/20/exploring-the-historic-trends-of-crypto-market-cycles-lessons-learned/

2. Unlocking your Inner Mogul: The Hidden Link Between Growth and Profit | https://www.mondaydaily.com/unlocking-your-inner-mogul-the-hidden-link-between-growth-and-profit/

3. "Hat Trick Hero: Score Motivational Goals for Victory" – A Guide to Achieving Success in Business and Life | pin-up: pin up casino login | pin up app | pin up casino app | pin up login. https://play-pinup-online.in/hat-trick-hero-score-motivational-goals-for-victory/

4. Embarking on the Entrepreneurial Journey: A Path to Personal Growth | Get Course. https://getcourse.com.au/blog/how-to-become-entrepreneur

5. https://www.questionai.ph/essays-e9FdEBtu2G3/debunking-myth-challenging-gender-stereotypes

6. https://fastercapital.com/topics/inspiring-stories-of-resilience-and-perseverance.html/3

7. https://muhammadsajwani.medium.com/resilient-employees-5-characteristics-7226269380b4

8. https://positivepsychology.com/resilience-in-the-workplace/

REFERENCES

9. https://muhammadsajwani.medium.com/resilient-employees-5-characteristics-7226269380b4

10. https://www.wishgram.com/message/resilience-in-the-face-of-challenges-guarantees-success-48154

11. https://www.wishgram.com/message/resilience-in-the-face-of-challenges-guarantees-success-48154

12. https://medium.com/@kkdhilipkumar0808/unlocking-your-full-potential-the-art-of-personal-growth-fa6163196b1e

13. https://fastercapital.com/topics/mental-toughness-and-resilience.html

14. https://www.classace.io/answers/suggest-practices-that-can-help-you-improve-your-self-esteem-providing-a-theoretical-explanation-to-support-your-answer

15. https://barrie360.com/reboot-goals/

16. https://jflowershealth.com/8-dimensions-of-wellness/#:~:text=A%20wellness%20wheel%20is%20a,a%20balanced%20and%20happy%20life.

17. https://www.clarion.edu/student-life/health-fitness-and-wellness/office-of-health-promotions/wellness-wheel.html#:~:text=The%20Wellness%20Wheel%20illustrates%20a,well%2Drounded%20and%20balanced%20lifestyle.

18. https://www.uwsp.edu/health/Pages/about/7DimensionsWellness.aspx

19. https://www.apa.org/topics/resilience

20. https://www.verywellmind.com/characteristics-of-resilience-2795062

21. https://www.govloop.com/community/blog/know-resilience-low/#:~:text=Risky%20Behavior%3A%20When%20our%20resilience,a%20vision%20for%20the%20future.

22. https://www.verywellmind.com/develop-an-internal-locus-of-control-3144943

23. https://repository.up.ac.za/bitstream/handle/2263/28568/02chapter3.pdf?sequence=3&isAllowed=y

24. https://www.viacharacter.org/survey/account/register

25. https://www.viacharacter.org/about

26. https://www.viacharacter.org/character-strengths

www.ingramcontent.com/pod-product-compliance
Lightning Source LLC
Chambersburg PA
CBHW051922160426
43198CB00012B/2001